AF574145
Judy Patricia Coghill

QUICKIE SEX

OVER 100 TRULY EXPLOSIVE TIPS

THIS IS A CARLTON BOOK

This edition published by
Carlton Books Limited
20 Mortimer Street
London W1T 3JW
Reprinted in 2009

A CIP catalogue record for this book is available from the British Library

ISBN 978 1 84222 556 1

Printed and bound in Malaysia

Editorial Manager: Judith More
Art Director: Penny Stock
Executive Editor: Zia Mattocks
Design: DW Design
Editor: Toria Leitch
Production Manager: Garry Lewis
Illustrator: Nicola Slater

QUICKIE SEX

OVER 100 TRULY EXPLOSIVE TIPS

LISA SUSSMAN

CARLTON
BOOKS

Minute One: **On Your Mark**

Let's face it, you're not always in the mood for some dreamy endless lovin'. Sometimes you're so damned hot you just want to fast forward past the Enya CD and the Tantric sex guidebooks and get on with the explosion.

The good news is that all it takes are five mad minutes to fire up your sex life big-time. That's right – 300 seconds. The fact is, there is nothing so exhilarating as fast, frenzied sex. Sex when you both have places to go, people to see, appointments to keep. Sex that is unplanned, impetuous and impulsive. Sex that borders on the forbidden or the foolhardy. Sex because you just have to have each other right here, right now.

Horny yet?
Then leave the dishes. Be late for work. And hold on to your hats – your sex drive is about to zoom from zero to 60 in less time than it takes to read this page.

7 REASONS TO DO IT RIGHT NOW

Having a quickie is essential for your mental health.

1

Stripped of all the trimmings, an orgasm is really just the physical release of built-up tension in the body. So quickies are a great way to de-stress (and much easier to get him to do than a massage).

2

Snagging a quickie is an instant mood lifter. Going fast and furious gets your blood flowing and boosts your endorphins for an oh-yeah booty bonus.

3

You jump-start your **inner sex goddess** by keeping your body pumped for action. According to research by Eileen Palace, PhD, the more stimulation your body receives, the more it is primed for being stimulated. So the more quickies you have, the more quickly you will get turned on.

4

A new way to spell relief: **Q-U-I-C-K-I-E**. According to research by Lawrence Robbins, MD, a dose of instant sex can help relieve women of pain from migraines (and it's a lot more energizing than a tranquillizer).

5

You're acting according to your biological nature. Humans were designed for fast sex, say evolutionary psychologists. The animal kingdom wasn't used to wasting time. The more time you spent copulating, the more vulnerable you were to being consumed by some woolly thing (and we don't mean your lover).

6

Quickies are efficient. They get the job done. So you get to have sex and still get a decent night's sleep at the end of it.

7

They're empowering. Yes, that's right. What could be more of a power trip than inciting your lover into a sexual frenzy?

4 REASONS HE WANTS YOU TO DO IT NOW

All it takes to plaster a goofy smile on his face is 5 minutes.

8

Men are suckers for a little mystery – studies show that the possibility of conquering the unknown is a top reason for why guys stray. Surprising him with some sex-on-the-run will stop him from thinking he knows all your secrets – keeping him as faithful as a St Bernard dog.

9

Research has found that an **occasional quickie** can be the answer to a lot of his sexual anxieties. There's no losing sleep over how long he has to last or whether he is giving you enough foreplay. All he has to do is get an erection and use it.

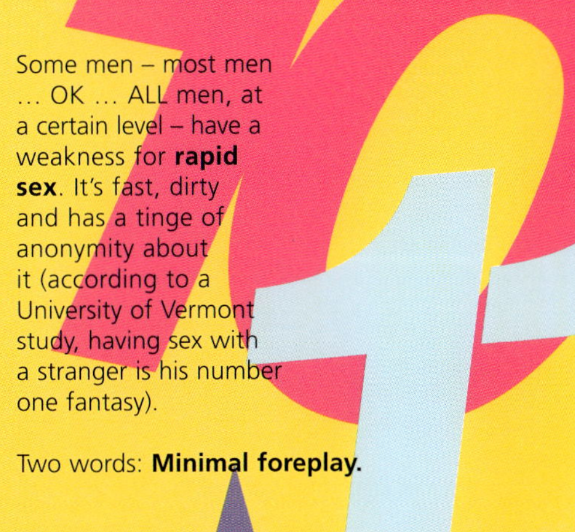

Some men – most men … OK … ALL men, at a certain level – have a weakness for **rapid sex**. It's fast, dirty and has a tinge of anonymity about it (according to a University of Vermont study, having sex with a stranger is his number one fantasy).

Two words: **Minimal foreplay.**

IF YOU'RE STILL NOT CONVINCED

7 MORE reasons why you really should do it now – if only to have a more bonded union.

Who has the time or energy for all the prep work that goes into prolonged sex? Dimming the lights to a flattering glow, burning candles, bracing yourself for the never-ending G-spot expedition … yawn. Sex is like dining. Sure, the five-course gourmet deal is delicious. But sometimes, nothing but a hamburger will do.

Even a tired quickie can convey **more tenderness and caring than long hours of lovemaking.** Bet this sounds familiar: You're exhausted. He wants sex. You love him so you don't want to reject him and you know you can do just about anything for five minutes (and chances are, once you get started, you'll find tip 66 kicking in).

While quickies may not be able to save a relationship in nosedive, they're certainly the easiest – and fastest – way to **revive a boring sex life.** If you're used to a certain method of making love, a fast body bash can break a ho-hum routine (and it beats dressing up in that French maid's outfit any day).

You'll keep the flames burning. Passion doesn't automatically keep going – you've got to work at it, say relationship psychologists. The role of a quickie is to turn up the heat once in a while.

Quite simply, **your relationship depends on it.** According to a study by Ellen Bersheid, PhD, a psychologist who researches close relationships, in order for love to thrive, it's essential that lovers experience minor interruptions so that they can recapture an awareness of their emotional involvement. Because you've behaved unexpectedly and interrupted a pattern (that is, your usual Saturday night making-love-in-bed), he'll be reminded of how much he loves you.

17

Nano-second sex reminds both of you that no matter how crazy life gets, there's always a little window of time to connect as a couple. (Three quickies a week is only 15 minutes. Anyone has time for that.)

18

The after effects last a long, long time. One poll found that couples who regularly speed up sex, kiss, cuddle and hold hands more. How's that for afterplay!

SO NOT TRUE

Take your time and read these quickie myths.

MYTH: Quickie sex bites.
TRUTH: Arousal is a mysterious and powerful thing, so the frantic abandon of a quick fix can ignite a climax that's every bit as explosive as a marathon session in the sack.

MYTH: Women need at least 72 hours of foreplay to have an orgasm.
TRUTH: Actually, cutting to the chase sexually can pay off passionately for both of you. The evidence shows that we don't exactly need a lot of time to experience sexual nirvana – according to studies by sex researchers Carol Darling, PhD, and Kenneth Davidson, women can, on average, reach orgasm in 8 minutes with a partner. In other words, full-blown, drawn-out foreplay, while tasty, is really just additional sauce.

MYTH: Women hate quickies.
TRUTH: Au contraire. In one survey conducted by Bowling Green State University, a group of men and women, aged between 25 and 43, were asked, 'If you had to make one choice – and you could have only one – which would you choose: hard, driving fast sex or slow, gentle sex?' The majority of the women wanted to get hammered.

222

MYTH: Languorous lovemaking, hours in bed, kisses and caresses that go on forever and back rubs are necessary for good sex.
TRUTH: You can be TOO relaxed. According to a Tulane University study, since orgasm is a tension release, the more STIRRED you are mentally during sex, the higher your bliss potential.

223

MYTH: If he wants a quickie, it means he doesn't love you.
TRUTH: Every act of sex doesn't have to be a relationship seminar. Studies show that couples who don't mind doing it quickly every once in a while have MORE sex because they don't place so much emphasis behind the meaning of each carnal moment together.

SECTION **TWO**

Minute Two: **Get Ready**

True, the great thing about a quickie is that it's pretty much a no-frills, anything goes proposition. There's no obsessing about setting the perfect mood, wearing the right lingerie or putting on clean sheets. For that matter, who needs sheets at all?

But the reality is that sex never happens spontaneously. If you expect it to, you're setting yourself up for disappointment. Generally, there's always a prelude that leads us to be sexual, say sex experts. A certain loving touch, a special outfit that gets us in the mood. Bottom line: whatever our preliminaries, we never come cold to sex, we always prepare.

So here are a few fast-and-loose guiding principles to prep you for chasing the World's Fastest Orgasm title. What are you waiting for?

ONE MINUTE TO BETTER WHOA!

Learn to exercise control.

Limber your love muscles. According to the American Association of Sex Educators, Counsellors and Therapists, toning your pubococcygeus (PC) muscles helps lubricate and stimulate you, making your orgasms come on more quickly and more intensely (this goes for men, too).

- Find the right muscles – the ones you use to stop your urine flow.
- Exercise them – squeeze and hold tight for three seconds. Relax for three seconds, then repeat, building up until you can maintain a squeeze for ten seconds. The more you do, the stronger the results.

25

No one will know what you're doing, so go ahead and **squeeze when you're stuck in a traffic jam,** you're bored at work or getting your hair done.

26

Bonus: Squeezing those PC muscles makes you aware of your vagina and clitoris, sending little turn-on messages to your body so you end up effortlessly doing tip 64.

27

To use during sex, squeeze as he slides out and release as he plunges in. It'll feel like a suction cup around his penis and create tantalizing friction for both of you.

30

A-SEX-ORIZE

How to dress for the occasion.

Plan on staying semi-clothed. If you're prepared to get naked, you're not impatient enough to get into the swing of the quickie (unless you're planning tip 78). Of course, ripping your clothes off is a different story.

Wear a suspender (garter) belt to work, you naughty thing. It'll give him access for later and get you into tip 64. No tights (pantyhose) unless you have a run in a strategic spot.

Slip into something new. According to one survey, husbands who fail to notice that their wives changed their hair colour from black to blonde literally leapt to attention at the sight of a fresh-off-the-rack pair of lace underpants or an unfamiliar push-up bra.

32

You don't have time to **worry about your body during a quickie.** So disguise your jelly belly with big panties that cut just above the belly button and make your stomach look flatter, a more practical solution than sucking in your breath.

Forget fashion and **slip into a longish, loose skirt** – it's ideal for hiking up and making a quick discreet connection in public places.

If you can't skip knickers altogether, **make them edible** (see tip 36 for buying info).

33 34 35

A sexy teddy or leotard that opens at the crotch will have you ready in a snap.

Y-fronts or boxer shorts for him were designed with a quickie in mind.

INTRODUCE A THIRD PARTY

There's nothing like your own personal joystick to get a buzz in a flash.

A Magic Wand vibrator, with a ball-shaped vibrating head, flexible neck and long cylindrical body is best for both of you (available on-line from www.annsummers.com).

37

Using a battery-operated vibrator will ensure that you don't run out of steam mid-play. According to the sex toy store Good Vibrations (www.goodvibes.com), the best are Japanese-made.

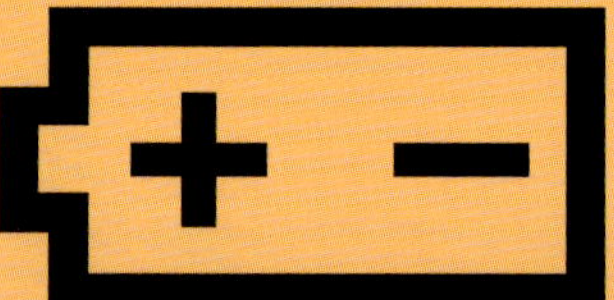

Best high-speed move: Press your new love toy against (not on) your clitoris or insert it into your vagina. Run it along the bottom side of the penis. Indirect vibes create a deeper, more satisfying orgasm than ones that hit your bulls-eye.

Woman-on-top and rear-entry positions allow plenty of room to get a good buzz going.

39

40

Pressing the head of the vibrator against your tummy will make you arch with ecstasy.

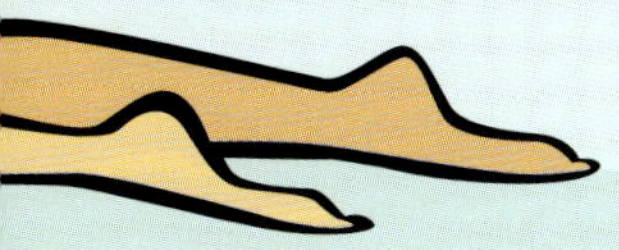

HURRY-UP HELPS

Tricks to heat the action up in a flash.

41 **Eat right.** Chocolate contains phenylethylamine, a mood-boosting chemical that can incite lust. Oysters are a good source of zinc, which studies show help his standing-to-attention powers. Other research suggests that seafood in general, which is high in protein, is also high in tyrosine, an amino acid that can act as a libido pick-you-up. And chilli peppers trigger the release of endorphins, feel-good brain chemicals that make you ready for action.

42 **Get wet.** Studies by sex researchers John Wincze, PhD, and Patricia Schriener-Engel, PhD, have shown our body's responses sometimes take time to catch up with our mental urges. Adding a drop of water-based lubricant to the head of the penis (or condom) before sex will keep your body and mind on the same sexy wavelength.

43

Forget crooners like Luther Vandross and Natalie Cole. A study from Loyola University discovered that heavy metal and other hard-rock variations get his pulses (and other bits) racing. So make sure you have a Limp Bizkit or Lincon Park CD in your collection.

Stick your schnoz in his underarm. A recent Bern University study found that this is where a whiff of someone's scent can send you into a sexual frenzy. A sniff of lavender and pumpkin pie will have the same stiffening effect on him – the Scent Smell & Taste Treatment and Research Foundation in Chicago discovered that these combined odours increase penile blood flow by 40 per cent.

44

45

Come – er – prepared. Studies on **easily orgasmic women** (those who climax more than 90 per cent of the time) have found that they often anticipate steamy encounters hours – even days – before (see tip 64 for suggestions).

46

You knew there had to be a good reason you were logging all those hours in tush-tightening class. A University of Washington study found **a quick 20-minute workout primes our bodies for sex** (and not just because we're at the gym ogling sweaty, buff men doing bench presses). It seems a hard-pumping heart sends blood to all extremities – including sex organs. So pump your own iron before you pump his.

47

Bump up your secret hot spot. Build sexual tension with this indirect pleasure prep: massage the area about one middle finger length below your belly button. Pressing it gently for about three minutes helps promote blood flow, firing up the whole pelvic area.

48

Keep a naked snap of your man (or anything you think looks really sexy) in your wallet. You'll feel flirty all day.

49

Carry a quickie kit:
Keep condoms, any props like scarves or handcuffs (for a little light bondage), lubrication and a compact mirror and hairbrush (for post-sex sprucing) to hand, so that in the midst of passion, you don't get stalled on technicalities.

PICK-YOU-UPPERS

Fuel up with the following to turn your libido into Speedy Gonzales.

50 According to studies, **fish and beans** can turn his wood from willow to mahogany.

51 Take a daily dose of libido-boosting **homeopathic remedies** like graphite, lycopodium or pulsatilla and say, 'Hubba-hubba'.

52 **Red wine** boosts testosterone levels to make your reactions raunchier – especially if you're on the Pill.

53

Give yourself an **energy boost.** Vitamin C energy powders will give you the orgasmic stamina you need for a quickie.

54

Get a buzz on with bee pollen. Research shows that it lifts energy levels, libido, sexual potency and fertility. How sweet it is!

Spicy foods such as chillies, garlic and onions ignite sexual passion. Just make sure you carry breath mints with you!

55

HOT AND BOTHERED

Give him THAT sign.

56 Simply take his fingers and **put them in your mouth**. It will send an instant message to his groin.

57 Get right to the point – lift up your top and **press your cleavage** against his back.

58 Try **blinking** in time to his breathing – it's like flashing the word SEX in front of his eyes.

Place his hands where you want them – on you.

Create a quickie code, perhaps a wink or a secret handshake that says in no uncertain terms **'You, me, here, now'**, to preclude any awkward misunderstandings or long, boring waits in the bathroom for an unwitting partner.

Stare directly at his **crotch.**

62

When you're out in a **public place,** disappear for a few minutes then, when you return, hand him your panties. Or whisper that you are wearing tip 33 in his ear.

63

Greet him naked.

Minute Three: **Get Set**

Here's a newsflash: he doesn't hold a patent on horniness. It seems that both men and women have a supply of the hormones that propel the sex drive into amorous action: oestrogen, progesterone and testosterone.

But there's more to keeping your sex drive in gear than pushing the right buttons or putting a tiger in your tank. To have all the heady force of a turbocharged engine in peak performance, your sex drive has to be revved emotionally as well as physically. That goes for men as well as women.

Here, then, is the owner's manual for getting your mind and body focused back to where it damn well should be – sex! Your car mechanic may not know about them, but these aids are a sure-fire guarantee for ignition.

MENTAL HURDLES

Having an orgasm is often 80 per cent mental and 20 per cent physical. Here's how to get in the right state of mind to enter the Oh! zone.

Sex up your brain. Fantasize or watch something sexy to get you in the mood (log on to www.nerve.com if you don't have any steamy video tapes to hand).

64

65 **Have a few drinks.** While studies show that booze inhibits men, it actually has the opposite effect on women (as long as you keep it to two).

66 **Think you are enjoying yourself and you will.** Even if it feels as if you're just going through the motions at first, it will feel great in just a minute. According to studies by sex researcher Eileen Palace, PhD, when women raise their expectations about sex (and think, 'of course my toes will curl'), their bodies become more responsive within 30 seconds.

67 **Get over it.** Sex doesn't cure cancer. It also doesn't ensure world peace or bring down superpowers. The point is, getting it right every time isn't that important. If you start fretting about whether you'll break sexual records, just start repeating to yourself: 'This feels good, this feels good' – in other words, forcing your mind to go with the flow of tip 66.

MASTER YOUR OWN DOMAIN

Give yourself a helping hand to remain in a sex-ready state.

68 **When masturbating,** women do not linger any longer than men: Kinsey reported that it takes an average of about three minutes for both to come to orgasm.

69 Studies have found that the **erotic highs** from masturbation can last a few hours. So you can speed things up by letting your fingers do the walking long before your lover arrives on the scene.

70 In one poll, 95 per cent of men said they like it when **their lover creates her own pleasure.** On one hand, it takes the pressure off them. On the other, it's just plain hot (if you really don't know why, see tip 95).

71 **Wet your fingers first.**

72 **Locate the target:** Touching the clitoris directly may be too intense, which means that instead of building up to an orgasm you may feel numbness or even pain. To avoid this, press your index and middle fingers on either side of outer lips, gently squeezing the fingers together in a circular motion to stimulate the clitoral ridge underneath.

73 **Squeezing and contracting** your thigh muscles while thrusting helps massage your clitoris against his hard body.

A QUICKIE FIX

Bed-tested techniques guaranteed to make the Earth move in sync.

You're Hot, He's Not: The quickest way to get a man hard is to go straight to the heart of the matter: his penis (a Pirelli calendar nearby doesn't hurt either). Three tips: use a firm grip, a wet hand and flick your tongue.

74

75

He's Hot, You're Not: You can waste time with him poking here and prodding there. But no one knows how to warm you up better than little ol' you. A little spit or lubrication on the finger will speed things along. Put your hand over his to make him putty in your hands (see tips 71 to 73 for beginner's help).

He Needs To Slow Down: According to the Kinsey Institute clock, a man can go from start to finish in one minute. To pace himself to last another 120 seconds, he can:

- Flex his muscles (when a man contracts his PCs – direct his attention to tip 24 – he can lower arousal a few notches).
- Breathe deeply (it directs blood away from his penis).
- Open his legs (when he is lying on top, he can spread his legs to take the pressure off his testicles – when they are too compressed, they become overstimulated.
- Change gears (simply changing positions can halt his momentum).
- Take it out (it removes him from the seat of action – blowing warm air onto it will keep him hot without exciting him to the point of no return).

76

77

You Need To Speed Up: Once a woman is hot, she can keep pace with any man. The trick is getting to the race on time:

- Begin without him (see tip 46).
- Let him help you get a head start with a one-minute visit south of the border (studies show oral sex has the double bonus of quickly lubricating and stimulating you in all the right places).
- Give yourself a helping hand (see tip 75).
- Position yourself correctly (getting on top will help his penis connect with your clitoris while rear entry is best suited for hands-on sex).

SECTION **FOUR**

Minute Four: **Go!**

With time at a premium, we're going to cut to the chase. Here, handy tips for doing the horizontal indoors, outdoors and everywhere in between.

Yes, it's risky. That's precisely the point. Moderate fear – not staring-down-an-agitated-lion fear but the kind you feel when you could potentially be caught doing something naughty – causes the production of adrenaline, the sexy pick-me-up you manufacture when you're aroused. But exercise discretion. While the other half of the thrill of a quickie is that the world, so to speak, is your mattress, you can be fined or arrested if caught.

GET YOUR TIMING RIGHT

When it comes to catching the orgasm express, timing is everything.

Skip lunch and have a nooner instead. Testosterone levels in adult males are subject to circadian rhythms, researchers have found, meaning that they rise and fall in 24-hour cycles – and they tend to peak shortly before 12 pm.

Your body starts screaming yes, yes, yes around mid-cycle (14 days after your last period) when oestrogen levels are at their highest.

Don't do it: **hold off having sex for two weeks** and it'll add instant heat to your flash-in-the-pan coupling.

Make a quickie your wake-up call. It's better than an alarm and the chances are, he'll already be hard.

81

LOCATION, LOCATION, LOCATION

Any where, any time, any place.

Concrete Jungle

Unless you're a masochist, if you're romping in an alley or on a road, you'll want minimal ground contact.

- For a raunchy position that stops your clothes from getting dirty and your bottom getting cold, he should **squat on his heels while you sit on his upper thighs facing him** with your weight on your feet. Wrap your arms around him for balance.
- Another hot move: Stand facing the wall with your feet about 45 cm (18 in) apart. **Standing facing your back with his feet between yours, he bends his knees and enters you from below.** Holding your hips to steady himself, he leans back while you lean forwards against wall, his hips pressed against your hips.

On the Move

Live life in the fast lane.

- **Do it on a roller coaster.** Studies show that screaming your head off on an amusement park ride causes a surge in adrenaline and endorphins, both of which give you a sexy thrill.
- **The seat belts in your car** can be used for light bondage at a pinch.

- If you indulge on the bonnet, **make sure the car alarm is off and the engine is cool.**
- Inside the car, **avoid unintentional pressing of the horn during the throes of abandonment** (drawing embarrassing attention to the vehicle) by jumping into the back seat. Another good car position is him sitting in the passenger seat with you on his lap facing him (if your legs are very long, you can rest them on his shoulders).
- While there's a lot to be said for a Porsche, according to the Petersen Auto Museum in Los Angeles, **the Volvo 70 Wagon is your best bet for quickie auto nookie** because of its frolic-friendly features: spacious, supple leather interior and rear seats that fold down to create a flat surface.
- **It's easy to hide a hand job under one of those little airplane blankets.** And if you're really sneaky, you can rest your head on your partner's lap and just happen to have oral sex. But try not to let your head bob up and down (unless there's turbulence).
- **Join the Mile High Club** (then you can register at www.milehighclub.com) by having sex on a plane once you reach cruising altitude. You can make a quick getaway to the toilet during the movie when there's usually no meal or beverage services. Face-to-face standing sex is best or he can enter you from behind (bonus: you can both watch in the mirror – see tip 96).

H2-Ohhh!

Make your own waves.

- **Hold on to your bikini bottoms.** You don't want to do the Walk of Shame back to your towel.
- The perfect pool or ocean water level is waist high (any lower and it's embarrassing, any higher and your passion may be swept away). **If you're surrounded by sunbathers, hold your breath and sink to the bottom,** pull your bikini bottoms to one side and let him perform oral thrill.
- **Have him stand up and enter you while you float on your back** – now try that when you're landlocked!
- In general, **the water needs to be quite warm so his erection won't sink.** However, the heat in a hot tub can cause blood vessels to dilate so his erection may not be as firm.
- While the beach seems movie-made for getting swept away, when sand gets in the creases and holds of the vagina, it can cause abrasions (think sandpaper), which makes it easier to catch STDs, including HIV.
- If possible, **have him enter you before you get wet and wild** so your natural wetness doesn't wash away first.

84

Going Green

Become a nature lover.

- Make use of the great outdoors. **Sunlight is additive-free Viagra.** One theory is that it makes people hornier because it suppresses their melatonin, a hormone believed to be the biological version of a five-course meal (in other words, it diminishes sexual desire). At the same time, it's speculated that sunshine increases serotonin and other hormones that make us more open to back-to-nature nookie.
- Do it in a cucumber patch – according to a study conducted by the Smell & Taste Treatment and Research Foundation, **the most arousing smell for women is cucumber** (lavender comes in second, great if you're in Provence).
- If passion overtakes you while you're walking in the woods, remember that mozzies love moist dark places – you get the picture (ouch!). **Spray yourselves with repellent before heading out.** A blanket or sleeping bag will also serve as barrier between you and any creepy crawlies.
- **Make sure you know what stinging nettles and poison ivy look like** (check out a website like www.vth.colostate.edu/poisonous_plants/).
- If you want extra wood, **choose a tree wider than your hips so it'll hold you up as you lean back against it.** If the bark is smooth, you can prop your bottom against it and wrap your legs around his waist so that it supports your weight.

85

On the Town

Make a break for it.

- **Hit the bathroom when you're at a restaurant.** The locked door won't arouse suspicion for at least 5 minutes (which is all you need). Also watching yourselves in the mirror as you go at it is pretty damned hot.
- **Go for the ladies' toilet,** as there is more privacy there than in the gents'.
- **If you do it in a dressing room, be careful about doing it against shoddy walls** (they may collapse). A changing bench or chair is much easier and won't arouse the suspicion of any curious salespeople.
- **You can have a quickie without leaving your table at a restaurant** if the tablecloth is long. Just use your big toe to masturbate each other.
- At the office, use a chair without wheels and flick on the computer monitor for sexy mood lighting (he sits and you perch on his lap).
- **If you're at a boring party, head for a tight closet.** He can squat on his knees while you lay on your back resting your knees on your chest and placing your feet on his torso. Start your motors. It's easy to get into and you get lots of deep thrusting.

87

GET IN POSITION

The top moves to master for playing beat-the-clock sex.

Standing Up:

- It can be tricky to match up your love organs if you're different heights, so face away from him and **bend over so that your hands are flat on the floor and your weight is forwards** (or lean against a wall). He simply enters you from behind. Because all you have to do is slip down your knickers (or just wear crotchless), you can take this show on the road – your office desk, the restaurant toilet, wherever the urge strikes.
- Tip 91 (the position for the stairs) will also even things out.
- If he's strong and you're light, try what the Kama Sutra calls suspended congress: **while he leans back against a wall, you face him, sitting on his joined-together hands (he should lace his fingers), with your arms around his neck.** You can move yourself by extending your legs and putting your feet against the wall.

Some moves are two-in-one:

- **Anything rear entry gives the deep penetration often needed with quick sex** and lets his penis hit the ultrasensitive front of your vaginal wall.
- If you're sitting in a chair, face away from him, as he can then also massage your clitoris. **Hooking your leg over the chair leg will create extra friction between your clitoris and his penis.**

- **Keep your legs together:** This straight-laced position can trigger an instant orgasm by making it easier to clench your thigh muscles, which continue far up enough to stimulate your inner clitoris (the tissue actually extends 9 cm (3.5 in) – about the length of your middle finger – up into the pelvic area).
- **Wear a girdle – sexy – yes!** It puts pressure on the lower abs, which stimulates your inner clitoris (see above). Or get him to use his hand – anything that presses down on the part of your abs just above your pubic mound (his hand, your hand, a stack of bricks) during intercourse should do the trick because it sandwiches your inner clitoris between the proverbial rock and a hard place – in this case, your tensed muscles and his penis. **Extra tip – make sure he's inside you first as it will be difficult for him to hit the mark otherwise.**

The door jamb: Make use of the entryways to both your body and home with this position (part of the appeal is you may get busted by neighbours or flat-mates). Caution: don't wear socks, it can make things uncomfortably slippery. **Find a narrow doorway. He leans backwards against the door jamb while you do the same with the other, straddling him.** You can figure out the rest.

The One-Minute: So-called because that's all he'll be able to hold it for unless he's Arnie Schwarzenegger. He sits down with his legs bent and his feet flat on the floor and his hands on the ground behind him. He pushes his bottom up off the floor, supporting his weight with his arms and legs. You mount, crouching over him, and ride off into the sunset (good for you're doing tip 82).

HOME SWEET HOME

Listen to your mother's advice: Get out of bed!

- **Have sex sitting on or leaning against a washing machine** during the spin cycle for an extra orgasmic spin.
- **The nozzle at your kitchen sink** will add new meaning to the phrase, 'getting hosed' when used during a quickie.
- Handy for sex in the kitchen or any other confined space is **sitting face-to-face and wrapping your legs around his waist** and your arms around his neck.
- **If you stop on the stairs,** stand one step higher to make penetration a snap.
- **Straight-back chairs give more room for manoeuvring.** You can sit on his lap facing away from him or wrap your legs around him facing him. Or kneel on the chair holding onto the back (though you may topple over if things get vigorous – which we hope they will).

Minute Five: **Oh!**

You might think that all it takes to have a quickie is a penis, a vagina and a few minutes. Not so fast.

Here is something you don't know: Erogenous zones – dense nerve endings – crackle all over the body, particularly in the earlobes, neck, palms, inner thighs and the backs of the knees. In one study, women were able to orgasm simply from having their arms stroked.

Men's and women's bodies have roughly the same landscape of nerve endings, meaning there's a whole continent of hot spots out there for the taking. The quickie is ideally suited for starting your pleasure expedition. Since you need to move quickly, here's your love map for increasing your thrill power in a hurry. Get ready to spin your orgasms into roargasms.

JUST DO IT

New 5-second tricks for packing 30 minutes of lovemaking into 5.

Talk dirty: Tell your lover what you want. Explicitly. Some suggestions: 'Mmm, squeeze my nipple. Harder. Yes, that feels so good' –- and so on. You get the idea. This isn't just to turn him on (though that's definitely a blissful side effect). But according to a Journal of Sex and Marital Therapy study, **women who can talk freely about sex have a higher degree of sexual satisfaction than those who can't.** Now that should get you saying 'Yes, yes, yes!'

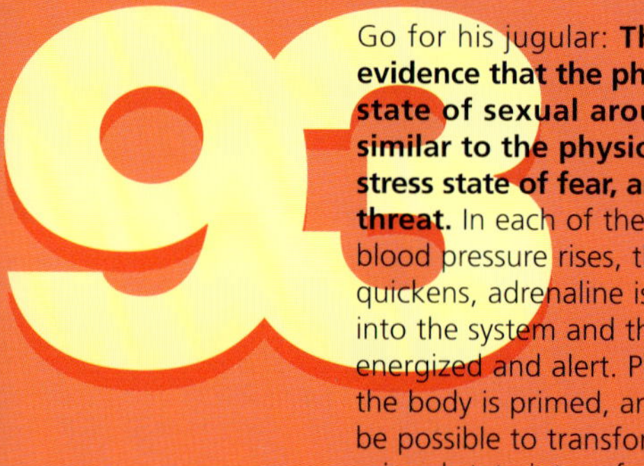

Go for his jugular: **There is evidence that the physiological state of sexual arousal is similar to the physiological stress state of fear, anxiety or threat.** In each of these states, blood pressure rises, the pulse quickens, adrenaline is released into the system and the body is energized and alert. Physically, the body is primed, and it may be possible to transform that primed state into a frenzy of sexual excitement.

Be selfish: Remember all that stuff your mother taught you about being polite? Forget it. This is no time to worry about the other guy. A quickie is every man and woman for himself and herself in a mad thrash for ecstasy. If you're thinking about pleasing him or he's thinking about satisfying you, then you're both missing the point. **Don't think about anything except giving yourself pleasure** (see tips 71 to 73 to get you on the me-me-oh-me road).

95

According to one poll, 40 per cent of men questioned are turned gooey by the natural scent of your nether regions. Not surprising since your vagina is a potent source of pheromones, chemicals that attract the opposite sex. Use it to your advantage – **touch your vagina and bring the scent to your partner's nose for a guaranteed turn-on.**

96

Use your eyes as well as your hands and mouth. A 1986 Archives of Sexual Behavior study reveals that both men and women are stimulated by erotic images, so keep the lights on and your eyes wide open.

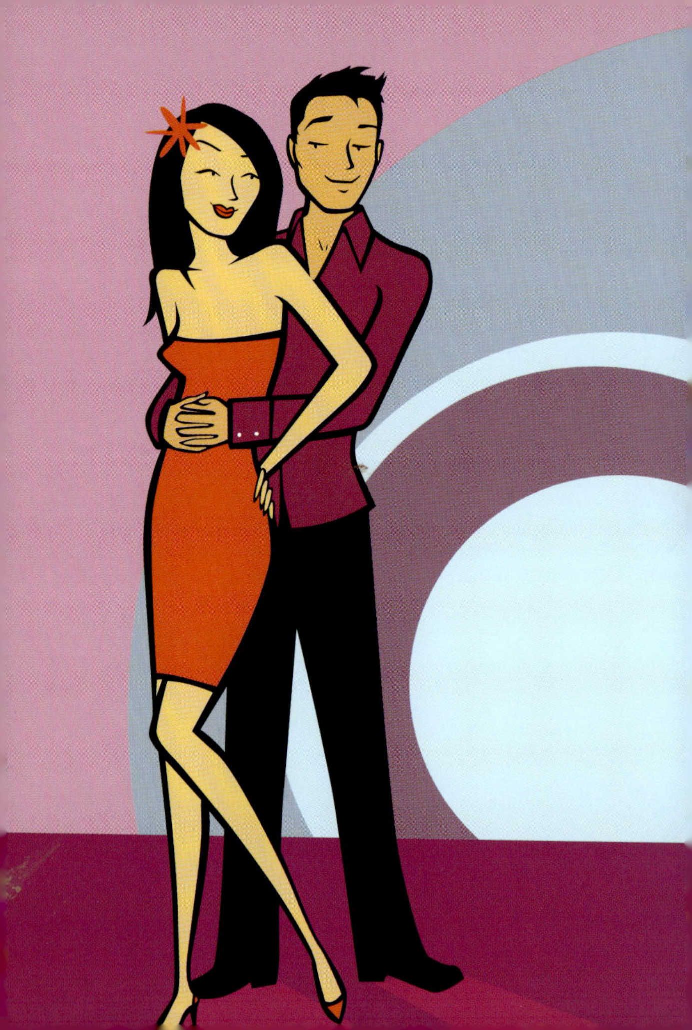

Pump up his passion by playing him a subliminally sensual tape of his favourite tunes (see tip 43 for which sounds to groove to). **Music actually activates the pleasure circuits of the brain** – the response can be so strong that it can even be orgasmic, according to a McGill University study on the subject.

97

98

Become a lady in red. **The colour crimson is reputed to amp up passion and enthusiasm,** so wear it when you want some feel-good fire.

LET YOUR FINGERS DO THE WALKING

To make the most of your time, here are a few pointers to keep at your (and his) fingertips.

99

Temples: Press your partner's temples and you'll feel veins throbbing. This pleasure point seems to have a direct link with the hypothalamus, your brain's bliss centre.

100

Ears: The cliché of blowing in your lover's ear is dead-on accurate. Stimulation from a darting tongue or a light, probing finger is such a powerful aphrodisiac that it can bring some men to orgasm. Researchers call the phenomenon the auriculogenital reflex and trace its origins to a nerve in the ear canal.

101

Mouth: When following tip 118, trace the outline of your partner's lips. He'll feel a familiar zing when you reach the comer of his mouth. This area is packed with rarely reached nerves just longing for some good loving.

102

Neck and spine: Try quick, playful love bites, especially on the ultra-sensitive collarbone. Move towards the centre of the back and trace the contours of the spine lightly with your tongue. Travel up and down your partner's back, blowing and tickling lightly as you go and watch him arch with pleasure.

Underarms: The tremendous accumulation of nerve endings here makes for great erotic potential. For a go-weak-at-the-knees move, use only your fingertips to stroke lightly and rhythmically from the rib cage towards the arms.

103

104

Nipples: You know that yours like attention, but so do his. Researchers have discovered that men's breasts have the same potential for erotic pleasure as women's breasts. In both sexes, the breasts are richly supplied with nerve endings, especially in the nipple area. Although only half as many men as women get hard nipples spontaneously when aroused, men's nipples are about as likely as women's to become erect when directly stimulated, and the sensation can sometimes make him explode.

Belly Button: Anthropologists call it a 'genital echo', meaning its shape reminds us of the vaginal opening, turning it into an instant visual turn-on. Heighten the carnal pleasure by probing it with a darting tongue while tracing the outline with your index finger.

Lower Belly: There is an erogenous connection between the belly button and pubic patch, marked out by a sensitive south-of-the-navel hairline. It will feel fantastic when stroked. Happy Trails.

107

107

Inner Thighs: This patch of land is ablaze with nerve endings because of the proximity to the genitals. Start with strokes so light that they barely register on your fingertips, and build to a crescendo of long, powerful strokes that work your fingers deep into the tender thigh muscles. Wowza.

108

Knees: The tender flesh behind the knee is good for both a tickle and a turn-on. Make sure your partner's leg is fully extended, then gently trace a figure-eight on the back of the knee with your fingertips or the tip of your tongue.

109

Fingers and Toes: Yes, it's true. Suck away. And don't forget to use your tongue to probe the crevices between each and every digit (on second thought, this might be best when doing tip 84 to keep things spic 'n span).

GOING DOWNTOWN

Measure for measure the muscle in your mouth holds more potential for pleasure than the one between your legs (and that goes for him, too).

110

Take a sip of water to **keep your mouth – and things – wet and shiny** (see tip 42).

Vary the temperature: Sip a hot drink or keep an ice cube in your mouth.

To speed things up, **let your mouth and hands work together.**

The flavour of your sexual marinade depends on your diet: Cow chompers have a pungent zest, vegetarians have a subtler flavour, spice lovers will pack a potent punch and the booze and ciggie brigade will have a slightly sour taste.

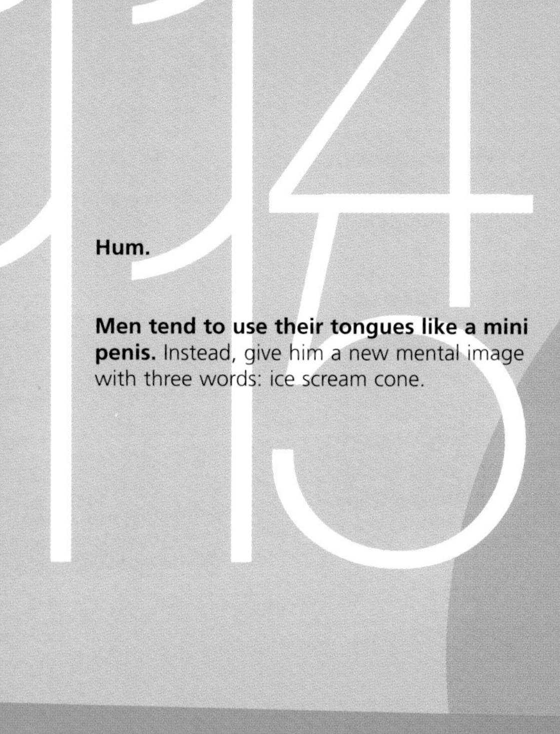

Hum.

Men tend to use their tongues like a mini penis. Instead, give him a new mental image with three words: ice scream cone.

A DIRECT HIT

Ultimately, you will need to focus – these sex-marks-the-spots are guaranteed to get your erotic juices flowing.

4 ways to work his penis (he'll be your love slave forever):

- **Don't rush when giving him a hand-job.** Going at warp speed will sometimes kill the sensation for him, so take it down a notch (in the time it takes to say 'Mississippi', you should go up and down about two times).
- Most women use a simple up-and-down stroke with the thumb pointing up for a hand-job. **Instead, start with the thumb pointing down and stroke up.** When you get to the head, flip your hand over and go down. Then switch to the other hand.
- The V-Spot: There's a V-shaped break in the ridge that runs around the head of his penis – **this is a small patch of skin can bring mind-blowing bliss** (just think of him stroking your clitoris).
- **The blood vessel-like seam on the underside of his penis that runs from just below the shaft to halfway down the scrotum is his scream seam.** Massaging it will directly massage his urethra – a supersensitive tube that is capable of registering intense pleasure.

Here's how to make it happen every time:

- On him: **Poke his perineum (the thumbnail-sized dimple just behind his scrotum).**
- On you: **Clitoris, clitoris, clitoris** – like the estate agents say, it's all about location. But there are also points inside the vagina that get hot when pressed – the G-spot (one-third of the way up the canal on the front wall), the AFE zone (another third up – stimulation of this spot also helps lubrication and sometimes leads to multiple orgasms) and the cervix (the lump-like opening to the uterus at the end of the canal).

SPEED BUSTERS

You can go from 1,000 to less than zero on the thrillometre in less time than it takes to say, 'Ouch'. Since you may not have time to restart your play, here's what to avoid in the first place.

118 **Not kissing first:** Avoiding the lips and diving straight for the erogenous zones gives the experience a pay-by-the-hour feeling where you're trying to get your money's worth by cutting out nonessentials. Of course, this may be the effect you're going for.

119 **Breaking contact:** The biggest downer to having a quickie is the lack of intimacy. Always keeping in touch with your partner's body makes a big difference. Move your hands together, or stroke them one at a time, in a continual flow. If you have to stop, keep one hand gently resting against your partner's body.

120

Not taking the extra minute to get hot and sweaty (see tip 42).

121

Yes, there's tip 21. **But you can still go too hard.** If he bashes his hip bones into your thigh or stomach, the pain is equal to two weeks of strenuous exercise concentrated into a few seconds.

122

Positioning yourselves incorrectly. The missionary position limits your clitoral stimulation, as well as your ability to move around beneath his body. Review tips 88 to 91 for the most spine- (and other bits) tingling moves on the run.

Giving a wedgie during foreplay. **Stroking gently through panties can be very sexy.** Pulling the material up between the thighs and yanking it back and forth in your rush to get on with the action is not.

123

124

Getting a non-battery powered vibrator (you don't want to waste precious minutes looking for a convenient outlet).

125

Forgetting, in your haste, to use any birth control.

CHEMISTRY

E. Preston, B.Sc.

Published by Intercontinental Book Productions in conjunction with Seymour Press Ltd

Distributed by Seymour Press Ltd., 334 Brixton Road, London, S.W.9

Printed in Great Britain by Unwin Brothers Limited
The Gresham Press, Old Woking, Surrey
A member of the Staples Printing Group

ISBN 0 85047 995 9

1.77.4

Contents

	Page
Introduction	5
Gas Laws	5
Molecular Weight of a volatile liquid	6
Structure—atomic and molecular. Bonding	7
Radioactivity	11
Energy including Born Haber cycle	11
Intermolecular Forces	15
Fractional Distillation, Steam distillation	18
Molecular Weights of non-volatile solutes	20
Abnormal molecular weights	24
Rate of reaction	25
Equilibria Kc, Kp, Solubility product	27
Electrochemistry—cells pH Buffers	31
Periodic Table—general points	36
Oxidation number	37
Group 1	38
Group 2	40
Group 3	42
Group 4	45
Group 5	47
Group 6	49
Group 7	53
Transition Elements	55
The mole. Molar Solution	60
Organic Chemistry—nomenclature	66
Isomerism	68
Organic Reactions	70
Hydrocarbons	71
Hydroxy compounds	77
Halides	80
Amines	82
Aldehydes and Ketones	84
Carboxylic Acids	87
Derivatives of Carboxylic acids	88
Polymers	92
Synthesis of Organic Compounds	95

Key Facts 'A' Level Books

Key Facts Books form the basis for examination answers, and cover the basic areas of each subject. They are ideal for a quick grasp of the subject and for revision, but should also be used as a reference throughout the course of study.

Key Facts Books are compiled by teachers who have detailed first-hand knowledge of examining and examinations in addition to their considerable classroom experience.

Key Facts Books are suitable for students studying for G.C.E. A Level or equivalent standard examinations.

Key Facts cover the most important parts of each subject syllabus for the various Examining Boards.

Key Facts Books enable a complete subject summary to always be carried in a pocket for learning in spare moments.

Key Facts Books make study time more productive, because time available can be spent actually learning from expertly produced material.

Remember that no-one can pass examinations for you. Success depends on how much effort **you** are able to make.

Learn the facts thoroughly. Regular review, throughout your course, is far better than last minute cramming. Try to work through one section each day. **Think** about the work. Try to **understand** it. Examiners look not only for understanding of the facts, but also for their inter-relationship and explanations.

Be sure to know your syllabus. Work through past papers to practise types of questions which are most often set. Use textbooks for fuller details if this seems necessary.

Always carry Key Facts Books with you,
and let them help you to Exam success.

Introduction

1. Examination syllabuses do vary. Ensure the requirements of the particular syllabus are known.
2. All note books and practical exercises should be revised thoroughly. This book aims to summarise the main aspects of an A level course but cannot cover all points of every syllabus.
3. It is often possible to do a calculation in more than one way. The methods used here are chosen because most students find them easy to follow.

Gas Laws

Boyle's Law
$P_1V_1 = P_2V_2$

Charles' Law
$V_1T_1 = V_2T_2$

Avogadro's Law Equal volumes of all gases under the same conditions of T and P contain equal numbers of molecules.

Graham's Law of Diffusion The rate of diffusion (R) of a gas is inversely proportional to the square root of the density (D) R = constant/D or $R_1/R_2 = \sqrt{D_1/D_2}$.

Dalton's Law of Partial Pressure The total pressure of a mixture of gases is the sum of the partial pressures of the constituent gases. The partial pressure is the pressure which would be exerted by the constituent if it alone occupied the total volume of the mixture.

General Gas Equation
$PV = RT$ for n moles of gas $PV = nRT$. R is gas constant.
Molar Volume of Gases. The volume occupied by 1 mole of any gas at S.T.P. is 22·4 dm^3.

$$\text{Vapour Density of a gas. } \frac{\text{The wt. of a vol. of gas}}{\text{Wt. of same vol. of hydrogen}}$$

$$\text{By Avogadro's Law. V.D.} = \frac{\text{Wt. of 1 molecule of gas}}{\text{Wt. of 1 molecule of hydrogen}}$$

$$\text{Also Molecular Wt. (M)} = \frac{\text{Wt. of 1 molecule of substance}}{\text{Wt. of 1 atom of hydrogen}}$$

$$\text{therefore V.D.} = \frac{\text{M Wt.}}{2}$$

Molecular Weight of a Volatile Liquid

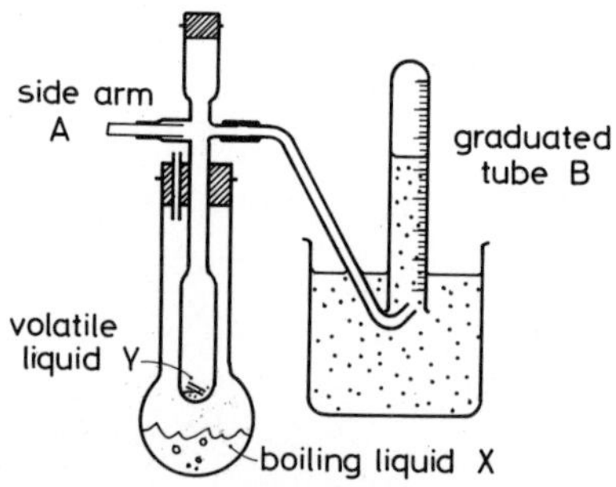

FIG. 1

Victor Meyer's Method The boiling liquid X expels air from the inner tube, when this stops the graduated tube is placed in position. The weighed Hoffman bottle containing the volatile liquid is dropped in through A. The liquid Y vaporises and displaces its own vol. of air V collected in B at atmospheric pressure and temperature t°C.

Example

0·136 g acetone displaced 55·3 cm³ of moist air measured at 13°C and 766 mm pressure. Calculate the molecular weight of acetone given that the saturated water vapour pressure at 13°C is 11·2 mm.

Pressure of dry air displaced $= 766 - 11{\cdot}2 = 754{\cdot}8$ mm

Volume of dry air displaced at S.T.P. $= 55{\cdot}3 \times \frac{754{\cdot}8}{760} \times \frac{273}{286}\,\text{cm}^3$

$= 52{\cdot}43\,\text{cm}^3$

52·43 cm³ acetone vapour at S.T.P. weigh 0·136 g.

22,400 cm³ acetone vapour at S.T.P. weigh $0{\cdot}136 \times \frac{22{,}400}{52{\cdot}43}\,\text{g} =$ **58·1**

(Note 1 mole of any gas at S.T.P. occupies 22·4 dm³)

Atomic Structure

	Charge	**Mass**	**Position**
Proton	+1	1	nucleus
Neutron	no charge	1	nucleus
Electron	−1	negligible	surrounding the nucleus.

Atomic Number is the number of protons in the nucleus of an atom. Since atoms are electrically neutral, the number of protons is equal to the number of electrons.

Isotopes are atoms of the same element having the same atomic number but different mass number due to variation in the number of neutrons.

e.g. Chlorine ^{35}Cl — 17p, 17e, 18n; ^{37}Cl — 17p, 17e, 20n

Determination of atomic mass

This is done most accurately using a mass spectrometer. A sample of the element is made to vaporise. The atoms produced are bombarded by electrons and hence form positive ions. The ions are accelerated by applying an electric field and then pass into an area where a magnetic field is applied. By changing the strength of the magnetic field ions of different mass can be brought to the detector and mass calculated from knowing the magnitude of the applied field.

Energy Levels

If the emission spectra of some elements are examined using a spectroscope, it is seen that each element has a characteristic set of lines. To explain these observations it is necessary to assume

(a) electrons in atoms can only exist in certain energy levels

(b) electrons can only jump from one energy level to another by absorption or emission of energy. This energy E is directly related to the frequency of radiation (μ) which causes the energy change. $E = h\mu$; h = Planck's constant.

Ionization energy

The first ionization energy of an element is the energy required to bring about the change $M(g) \rightarrow M^+(g) + e$ per mole. The first ionization energy of the elements Li—Ne varies in exactly the same way as that of the elements Na—Ar.

This periodic variation of first ionization energy is explained by assuming that (i) **there is a maximum number of electrons which can be contained in any particular energy level.** (ii) **electrons which are highest in energy are lost first.**
Each sub level has one or more orbitals which can accommodate two electrons which spin in opposite directions. Where more than orbital is associated with a particular sublevel electrons fill up the orbitals singly before pairing begins. (Hund's Rule.)

	↓↑	↓↑	↓	4p		
	↓↑	↓↑	↓↑	↓↑	↓↑	3d
$n=4$	↓↑	4s				
	↑↓	↑↓	↑↓	3p		
$n=3$	↑↓	3s				
	↓↑	↓↑	↓↑	2p		
$n=2$	↑↓	2s				
$n=1$	↑↓	1s				

Electronic structure of bromine $1s^2 2s^2 2p^6 3s^2 3p^6 3d^{10} 4s^2 4p^5$
The electronic configuration of an atom may be represented by using the above notation. Examples: sodium $1s^2 2s^2 2p^6 3s^1$, fluorine $1s^2 2s^2 2p^5$, iron $1s^2 2s^2 2p^6 3s^2 3p^6 3d^6 4s^2$ (4s level is lower in energy than 3d level and hence fills in first).

STRUCTURE OF CRYSTALS

The structure of crystalline solids can be elucidated by X ray diffraction. The X rays interact with the electrons of particles of atomic size and are scattered by them. The scattered waves may reinforce each other or neutralize each other. If X rays fall on to a crystal where the atoms or ions are arranged in regular layers conditions for reinforcement may be calculated using the Bragg equation $2d \sin\theta = n\lambda$.
If the angle at which reinforcement occurs (θ) is measured for X rays of known wavelength (λ) the distance between the lattice planes (d) can be calculated. This procedure must be repeated for different sides of the crystal.
Note. The X rays are in fact diffracted by the layers but they behave as if they were reflected and Bragg's equation is derived on this assumption.
X ray diffraction gives information as to the arrangement of molecules

or ions in a crystal and also the position of atoms in the molecule or ion. Hydrogen atoms have insufficient electron density to be detected.

BONDING BETWEEN ATOMS

Ions

When electrons are transferred from one atom to another, ions are formed. Whether or not an atom will form an ion can be decided by applying **Fajan's rules** which say that an ion is formed most easily if (i) the charge on the ion is small, (ii) the electronic structure of the ion is stable, (iii) if the anion is formed from a small atom and the cation from a large atom.

Ionic crystals e.g. NaCl, KI
The ions are held together by electrostatic forces which are very strong and considerable energy is necessary to overcome them—hence high melting and boiling points.

Covalent bonds

A covalent bond is formed by the sharing of a pair of electrons. Often an electron is provided by each atom e.g. methane CH_4

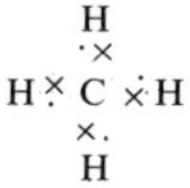

```
     H
     ·×
H ×· C ×· H
     ×·
     H
```

but if both electrons are provided by same atom then this is called a dative covalent bond.

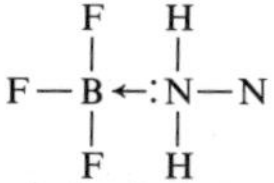

```
    F    H
    |    |
F — B ←: N — N
    |    |
    F    H
```

The arrow indicates that the pair of electrons is being provided by the other atom.
A dative covalent bond is still a covalent bond and may be written—
Bond polarization arises where a pair of electrons is shared between two atoms one of which is more electronegative than the other. Some ionic character is apparent e.g. H—Cl. Chlorine is more electro negative than hydrogen, and the electrons are drawn more towards the chlorine atom than the hydrogen atom. This gives rise to a slight negative charge on the chlorine atom and the hydrogen atom is therefore slightly positively charged $H^{\delta+}$—$Cl^{\delta-}$.

Molecular crystals e.g. solid carbon dioxide, iodine.
The molecules are arranged in a definite pattern in the lattice but are held together by weak van der Waal's forces. Little energy is needed to overcome these and molecular crystals have low melting and boiling points.

Atomic crystals e.g. diamond, graphite.
The atoms are held in the lattice by very strong covalent bonds and hence have high melting and boiling points.

Metallic bonds

Metals conduct electricity indicating there are free electrons. These electrons are **delocalized**. A simplified picture of the structure of a metal is of a series of positive ions (formed by the loss of the delocalized electron) surrounded by a pool of electrons. The attraction between the positive ions and the electrons constitutes the metallic bond.

Shapes of molecules

Molecules or ions containing covalent bonds have definite shapes. The bonding pairs of electrons and lone pairs, if any, repel each other and therefore arrange themselves as far as possible from one another. Lone pairs of electrons repel each other more strongly than bonding pairs and the bond angle is smaller than usual in molecules containing lone pairs.

Examples

2 bonding pairs	$BeCl_2$	linear	bond angle	180°
3 bonding pairs	BCl_3	planar	bond angle	120°
4 bonding pairs	CH_4	tetrahedral	bond angle	109·5°
3 bonding pairs, 1 lone pair	NH_3	tetrahedral	bond angle	107°
2 bonding pairs, 2 lone pairs	H_2O	tetrahedral	bond angle	104°

The bond angle in ammonia is less than the usual tetrahedral bond angle due to the greater repulsive effect of the lone pair. In water the bond angle is further reduced since there are two lone pairs of electrons and lone pair, lone pair repulsion is more effective than lone pair, bonding pair repulsion.

Radioactivity

Radioactive substances spontaneously emit radiation which is independendent of temperature and pressure. These rays affect a photographic plate, ionise gases, harm living cells and make zinc sulphide flouresce. There are three types of rays emitted. (i) α-rays. These consist of a stream of positively charged helium nuclei $^{4}_{2}He$. The superscript refers to the mass number (atomic weight), and the subscript to the atomic number. They have little penetration. (ii) β-rays. These are more penetrating than α-rays and consist of streams of fast moving electrons. (iii) γ-rays. These are electro-magnetic radiations of very high frequency, (similar to x-rays).

Spontaneous Disintegration The nucleus of a radioactive substance is unstable and disintegrates spontaneously to form a stable nucleus, eventually Pb, i.e. all elements with a higher atomic number than lead are radioactive.

(i) When α-particles are emitted, the nucleus loses 2 protons and 2 neutrons, i.e. the atomic number is decreased by 2 and the atomic weight by 4. (ii) A neutron can be considered to be a combination of an electron and a proton. If the β-particle (electron) is emitted, this leaves an extra proton in the nucleus, i.e. the atomic number is increased by 1 and the mass is virtually unchanged. There are three naturally occuring disintegration series, uranium, thorium, and actinium e.g. Uranium Series.

$$^{238}_{92}U \xrightarrow{\alpha} {}^{234}_{90}Th \xrightarrow{\beta} {}^{234}_{91}Pa \xrightarrow{\beta} {}^{234}_{92}U \xrightarrow{\alpha} {}^{230}_{90}Th$$

and so on to $^{206}_{82}Pb$ (stable).

The rate of decay is directly proportional to the amount of material present, therefore the time taken for the radioactivity to fall to a half its value is a constant for each substance. This is the **half life.**

Artificial Transmutations It is possible to change one element into another by bombarding it with fast moving neutrons, protons, α-particles and deuterium nuclei, e.g. an atom of nitrogen when subjected to a stream of fast moving α-particles is changed into an isotope of oxygen and a proton.

$$^{14}_{7}N + {}^{4}_{2}He \rightarrow {}^{17}_{8}O + {}^{1}_{1}H$$

Energy

If in a chemical reaction, the total energy of the products is less than that of the reactants, the reaction is **exothermic** i.e. energy is given out. If the energy of the reactants is less than that of the products, the reaction is **endothermic** i.e. energy is taken in.

The **heat of formation** of a compound is the heat evolved or absorbed when one mole of the compound is formed from its elements in their standard states. It is often symbolised as ΔH_f^θ which refers to the standard heat of formation at a temperature of 298 K and at a pressure of 760 mm mercury.

The **heat of combustion** of a substance is the heat evolved when one mole of a compound is completely burnt in oxygen.

The **heat of atomization** of an element is the heat absorbed when one mole of gaseous atoms is formed from the element.

The **heat of neutralization** of an acid or base is the heat evolved when one mole of hydrogen ions (more correctly H_3O^+) or one mole of hydroxyl ions is neutralized.

Hess's Law states that the heat evolved or absorbed during a chemical change is independent of the route taken.

INDIRECT METHODS FOR FINDING HEATS OF FORMATION

If the heats of combustion of the compound and its constituent elements are known, the heat of formation of the compound can be found by applying Hess's Law.

e.g. The heats of combustion of carbon and carbon monoxide are $-393\ \text{kJ mol}^{-1}$ and $-283\ \text{kJ mol}^{-1}$ respectively. Find the heat of formation of carbon monoxide.

$$C + \tfrac{1}{2}O_2 \xrightarrow{\Delta H_f} CO$$

$$\Delta H_1 + \tfrac{1}{2}O_2 \downarrow \qquad + \tfrac{1}{2}O_2 \swarrow \Delta H_2$$

$$CO_2$$

Using Hess's Law, $\Delta H_f + \Delta H_2 = \Delta H_1$

$$\Delta H_1 = -393\ \text{kJ mol}^{-1}$$

$$\Delta H_2 = -283\ \text{kJ mol}^{-1}$$

$$\therefore \Delta H_f - 283 = -393$$

$$\Delta H_f = -393 + 283 = -110\ \text{kJ mol}^{-1}$$

CALCULATION OF HEATS OF REACTION

Standard heats of formation can be used to find the heat change or enthalpy change which takes place in a reaction. e.g. The heat of formation of lead II oxide is $-219\,kJ\,mol^{-1}$ and that of water $-286\,kJ\,mol^{-1}$. Find the enthalpy change of the reaction (ΔH_f^θ for all elements is zero)

$PbO(s) + H_2(g) \rightarrow Pb(s) + H_2O(l)$

If an energy cycle is constructed

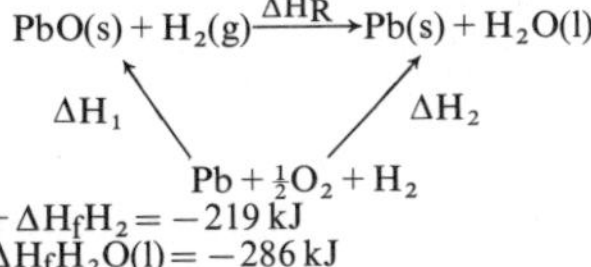

$\Delta H_1 = \Delta H_f PbO + \Delta H_f H_2 = -219\,kJ$

$\Delta H_2 = \Delta H_f Pb + \Delta H_f H_2O(l) = -286\,kJ$

By Hess's Law

$\Delta H_1 + \Delta H_R = \Delta H_2$ since the total heat change is independent of the route taken (Hess's Law).

$\therefore -219 + \Delta H_R = -286$

$\Delta H_R = -286 + 219 = -67\,kJ$

BOND ENERGY

A Bond energy is the energy associated with a particular bond. This may vary somewhat depending on other bonds in the molecule and it is the average bond energy which is used. Given that the bond energy for (C—H) = $+412\,kJ\,mol^{-1}$, (C—O) = $+360\,kJ\,mol^{-1}$, (O—H) = $+464\,kJ\,mol^{-1}$ and (C—C) is $+348\,kJ\,mol^{-1}$, calculate the energy needed to atomize one mole of ethanol in the gaseous state.

```
    H   H
    |   |
H — C — C — O — H
    |   |
    H   H
```

5 C—H bonds = 5 × 412 = 2 060 kJ
1 C—C bond = 1 × 348 = 348 kJ
1 C—O bond = 1 × 360 = 360 kJ
1 O—H bond = 1 × 464 = 464
Total heat required = 2 060 + 348 + 360 + 464 = 3 232 $kJ\,mol^{-1}$.

BORN HABER CYCLE

Sodium and chlorine combine together and yet the ionization energy required to form Na^+ is not balanced by the electron affinity of chlorine. The other factor involved is the **lattice energy.** This is the energy evolved when one mole of crystalline sodium chloride is formed from sodium and chlorine ions in the gaseous phase.

$Na^+(g) + Cl^-(g) \rightarrow Na^+Cl^-(s)\ \Delta H = \text{lattice energy.}$

Lattice energy cannot be measured directly but calculated from an energy cycle known as the Born Haber Cycle. Considering the reaction between sodium and chlorine

$Na(s) + \frac{1}{2}Cl_2(g) \rightarrow NaCl(s)\ \Delta H = -411\ kJ\ mol^{-1}$

This is the heat of formation of sodium chloride.

This same process can be split into several stages and the total energy for these stages must also be $-411\ kJ\ mol^{-1}$. The stages involved are

(i) atomization of sodium $Na(s) \rightarrow Na(g)\ \Delta H = +m\,kJ$

(ii) ionization of sodium $Na(g) \rightarrow Na^+(g) + e\Delta H = +n\ kJ$

(iii) atomization of chlorine $\frac{1}{2}Cl_2(g) \rightarrow Cl(g)\ \Delta H = +p\ kJ$

(iv) electron affinity of chlorine $Cl(g) + e \rightarrow Cl^-(g)\ \Delta H = -q\ kJ$

(v) lattice energy $Na^+(g) + Cl^-(g) \rightarrow NaCl(s)\ \Delta H = L.E.$

Thus $(m+n+p-q+L.E.) = -411$

$$L.E. = -411 - (m+n+p-q)$$

This is usually expressed in a diagramatic form.

Solvation energy

This is the energy evolved when the following change occurs

$M^+(g) + X^-(g) \rightarrow M^+(aq) + X^-(aq)$

It is this energy which accounts for the fact that most crystalline solids have a small heat of solution yet have a large lattice energy.

$M^+Cl^-(s) \rightarrow M^+(aq) + Cl^-(aq)\ \Delta H = \text{heat of solution}$

This change can occur in two theoretical stages

(i) $M^+Cl^-(s) \rightarrow M^+(g) + Cl^-(g)$
which requires energy (x kJ) equal to the lattice energy.

(ii) $M^+(g) + Cl^-(g) \rightarrow M^+(aq) + Cl^-(aq)$

$\Delta H = $ solvation energy ($-y$ kJ) (hydration energy).

Heat of solution = lattice energy with + sign + hydration energy

$$x\ kJ + (-y\ kJ)$$

MIXTURES OF LIQUIDS

If certain liquids are mixed in equimolar proportions, the boiling point of the mixture is approximately the mean of the boiling points of the two liquids in the mixture. Such liquids are usually of similar structure e.g. two hydrocarbons, two isomeric alcohols. However if two liquids having quite different structure are mixed e.g. acetone and trichloromethane the relationship between the boiling point and the composition of the mixture is not linear.
Raoult's Law states that for a mixture of liquids, the partial vapour pressure of each component is proportional to its mole fraction in the mixture. Mixtures which obey Raoult's Law are called **Ideal solutions.** The vapour pressure of a liquid at a given temperature is the pressure exerted by the vapour when it is in equilibrium with the liquid. For a mixture of two ideal solutions A and B

$$\frac{\text{partial vapour pressure of A}}{\text{vapour pressure of mixture}} = \frac{\text{number of moles of A}}{\text{number of moles of (A+B)}}$$

Relationship between V.P. and boiling point

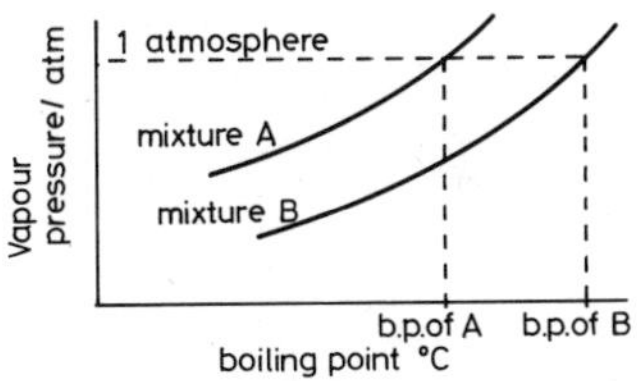

FIG. 2

It can be seen from the graph that a decrease in vapour pressure results in a proportional increase in boiling point.

Deviations from Raoult's Law

If the vapour pressure of the mixture is greater than that predicted for an ideal solution, this is called a positive deviation from Raoult's Law and the boiling point of the mixture is less than predicted.

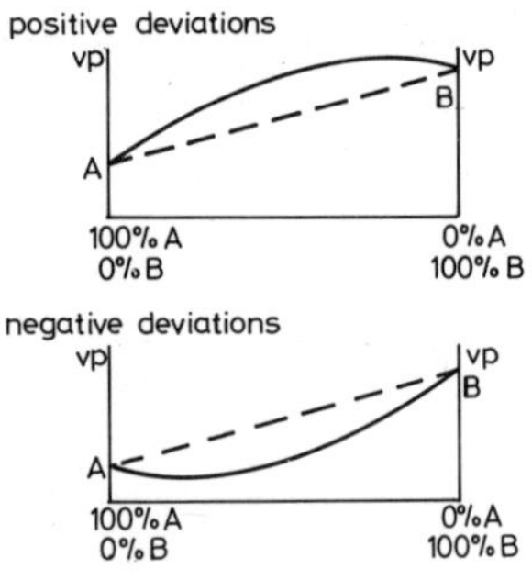

FIG. 3

Explanation of deviation

Negative deviations from Raoult's Law may be interpreted in terms of new bonds being formed between the molecules making their escape from solution more difficult. Thus the vapour pressure is lowered and the boiling point of the mixture higher. In this case acetone and trichloromethane:

$$\mathrm{Cl}-\underset{\mathrm{Cl}}{\overset{\mathrm{Cl}}{\underset{|}{\overset{|}{\mathrm{C}}}}}-\mathrm{H}\cdots\mathrm{O}=\mathrm{C}\begin{matrix}\diagup \mathrm{CH_3}\\ \diagdown \mathrm{CH_3}\end{matrix}$$

a hydrogen bond is formed.

On the other hand, if the molecules of one liquid are already hydrogen bonded as in ethanol, then the addition of hexane will result in an increase in vapour pressure (+ deviation) since the cyclohexane molecules interfere with the hydrogen bonds between the ethanol molecules making it easier for the molecules to escape. Bond breaking which occurs here is reflected in a decrease in temperature which occurs when such liquids are mixed i.e. energy required to break bonds and therefore endothermic reaction. In negative deviations where bonding occurs, mixing is accompanied by a rise in temperature i.e. bond formation is exothermic.

Hydrogen bonding

1. See deviation from ideal behaviour.
2. If the boiling points of the hydrides of the elements in groups 5, 6 and 7 are examined it will be noticed that ammonia hydrogen sulphide and hydrogen fluoride have boiling points which are much higher than would be expected from the trends in the rest of the groups. This indicates there must be considerable attractions between the molecules and hydrogen bonds occur.

```
                         H
                          \
e.g.  H—F···H—F            O···H
                          /     \
                         H       O
                                /
                               H
```

In ice the water molecules form a lattice being bonded by hydrogen bonds.
3. The molecular weight of acetic acid if determined in aqueous solution is 60 but if dissolved in benzene, the molecular weight is 120. This indicates that in benzene the molecules exist as dimers being held together by hydrogen bonds.

```
             O···H—O
           //       \
     CH3—C           C—CH3
           \        //
             O—H···O
```

In water, the acetic acid molecules are hydrogen bonded to the polar water molecules rather than to each other.
4. Substances which are able to form hydrogen bonds with the water molecules are likely to be soluble in water e.g. sugar has a large number of –OH groups in each molecule making hydrogen bonding with water molecules easy and considerable.

Van der Waal's forces

These are weak forces of attraction. The larger the number of electrons in an atom the greater the van der Waal's forces and these may be responsible for the rise in boiling point in the alkanes rather than simply to the increase in size of the molecules. If two isomers of an alkane are considered, the straight chain isomer has the higher boiling point. In the linear molecule there is an extensive surface area for contact with other molecules making more van der Waal's forces possible and hence a higher boiling point than in the branched isomer where there are fewer van der Waal's forces.

Solutions of Liquids in Liquids

Boiling Point Composition Curve for Two Miscible Liquids

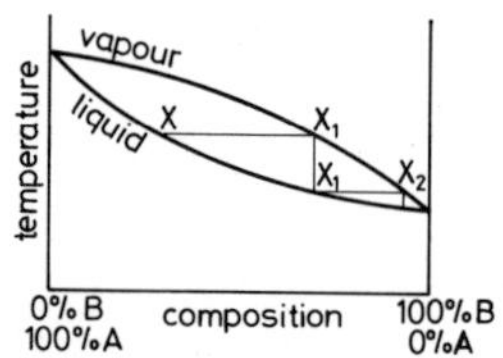

FIG. 4

Fractional Distillation

When two miscible liquids are distilled the vapour evolved contains a higher proportion of the more volatile constituent as shown in Fig. 4. A mixture which shows the above characteristics can be separated by fractional distillation, e.g. if a liquid of composition X is boiled then it will produce a vapour of composition X_1, which on condensation will give a liquid of the same composition (X_1), i.e. on one distillation the liquid produced is richer in the more volatile component B. If the liquid is now repeatedly vaporised and condensed it will give practically pure B. A fractionating column is a device which enables these repeated distillations to be carried out in one piece of apparatus. The vapour is condensed at each plate and this liquid is vaporised by the hot gas rising from below, e.g. Acetone and water.

Steam Distillation

For completely immiscible liquids the vapour pressure is equal to the sum of the separate V.P.'s of the components. As the mixture will boil when the V.P. is equal to the external pressure it follows that such a mixture will boil at a lower temperature than either constituent.

CONSTANT BOILING MIXTURES

If the boiling point composition curve for the liquids shows a minimum or a maximum then a constant boiling mixture is produced on distillation. Such a solution cannot be separated by fractional distillation.

(i) **Minimum Constant Boiling Mixture** C_2H_5OH/H_2O

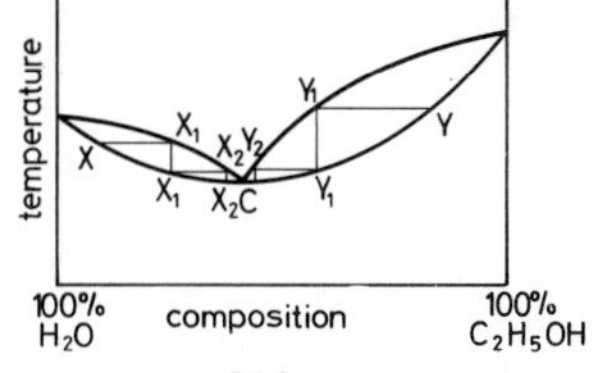

FIG. 5

When a liquid of composition *X* is distilled it will eventually produce a vapour of composition *C*. At this point the liquid and vapour compositions are equal, no further separation can occur. Similarly when a liquid of composition *Y* is fractionally distilled it will give the same result i.e. a mixture of constant composition boiling at a constant temperature.

(ii) **Maximum Constant Boiling Mixture** HCl/H_2O

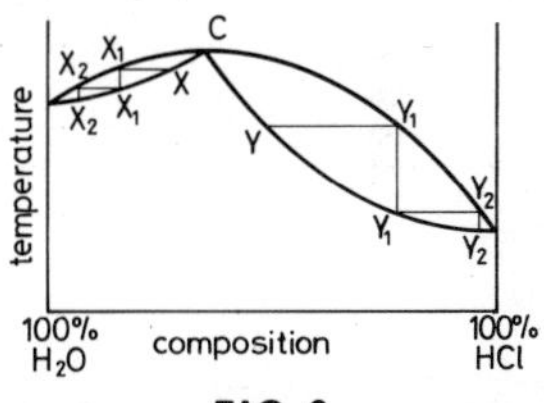

FIG. 6

When a liquid of composition *X* is fractionally distilled it will eventually give pure steam. The percentage of HCl in the remaining liquid will increase until at *C* a constant boiling mixture is formed. If a solution of composition *Y* is distilled then eventually pure HCl will be given off and the resulting liquid becomes richer in H_2O until composition *C* is reached. Again at *C* the liquid and the vapour have the same composition.

Molecular Weights of non-volatile solutes

Raoult's Law may also be stated as—the relative lowering of the vapour pressure (V.P.) of a solution containing a non-volatile solute is equal to the mole fraction of the solute in the solution. If p_o is V.P. of pure solvent, p V.P. of solution n, number of solute molecules, N, number of solvent molecules then:

$$\frac{p_o - p}{p_o} = \frac{n}{N+n} \simeq \frac{n}{N}$$

for dilute solutions N+n approx. N. The law applies only to (i) dilute solutions, (ii) non-volatile solutes, (iii) no dissociation or association, (iv) no reaction between solute and solvent.
If W_1 is the weight of solute and W_2 the weight of solvent and M_1 the mol. weight of solute and M_2 the mol. weight of solvent then:

$$\frac{p_o - p}{p_o} = \frac{W_1 . M_2}{W_2 . M_1}$$

p, p_o are very difficult to measure accurately so this method is not used directly.

DEPRESSION OF FREEZING POINT (ΔT_F)
ΔT of a solution is proportional to the lowering of the V.P.
$\Delta T = k(p_o - p)$

From Raoult's Law $p_o - p = \frac{n}{N} p_o$

$$\therefore \Delta T_F = kp_o \frac{n}{N} = k_1 \frac{n}{N} = \frac{k_1 W_1 M_2}{W_2 M_1}$$

For a constant weight of solvent $\frac{W_2}{M_2}$ is constant

$$\therefore \Delta T_F = \frac{k_2 W_1}{M_1} = \frac{KW}{M}$$

If the weight of solvent is 1 000 g, then k_2 is the **Cryoscopic Constant K.** W is the weight of solute in 1 000 g of solvent and M is its mol. weight. K is the theoretical depression obtained when 1 mole of any solute is dissolved in 1 000 g of solvent,
e.g. for H_2O, K = 1·86°C per mole.

Determination of ΔT_F and hence M
The Beckmann Thermometer (T) is set near the top of the scale and the freezing point of a known weight of solvent found. The solvent is then allowed to melt and a weighed amount of solute in pellet form is introduced through A. The freezing point of the solution is found as above and hence ΔT_F. Hence calculate M.

N.B. (i) It is absolutely essential that the liquid in *B* is continually stirred throughout the experiment.
(ii) The lowest temperature recorded will not be the freezing point because of supercooling, this is taken when the temperature is steady.
(iii) The pure solvent must freeze out alone.

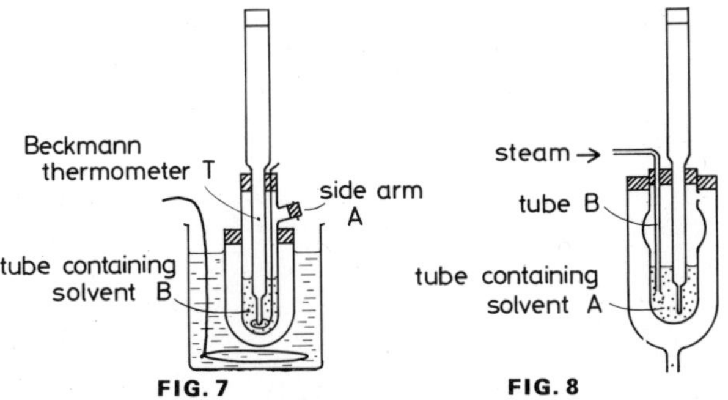

FIG. 7 FIG. 8

Elevation of boiling point (ΔT_B)
Since the ΔT_B is proportional to $p - p_o$. $\Delta T_B = \frac{KW}{M}$

K – the **Ebullioscopic constant**
T is set near the bottom of the scale, and a convenient vol. of solvent placed in *A*. Steam is passed through *B* until the solvent boils and the boiling point is taken. A known weight of solute in pellet form is added and the boiling point found as above, giving ΔT_B.
The vol. of solution is measured in *A* and assuming it has the same density of solvent calculate W. Hence find
M from $M = \frac{KW}{\Delta T_B}$

N.B. Superheating is avoided by the method of heating with steam.

OSMOTIC PRESSURE

Osmosis The name given to the flow of solvent molecules from a dilute solution to a more concentrated one, when separated by a semi-permeable membrane (or from a solvent to a solution).

Semi-permeable Membrane Allows the passage of solvent molecules only.

Osmotic Pressure (Π) The excess pressure required to prevent osmosis when a solution is separated from pure solvent by a semi-permeable membrane.

Laws. (i) At constant temperatures the osmotic pressure of a solution is proportional to the molecular concentration (C) of the solute $\Pi \propto C$.

(ii) For a given solution the osmotic pressure is proportional to the kelvin temperature, $\Pi \propto K$.

(iii) A solution containing 1 mole of solute in 22·4 cubic decimetres of solution exerts an osmotic pressure of 1 atmosphere at 0°C. Combining (i), (ii) and (iii)

$$\frac{\Pi_1}{C_1K_1} = \frac{\Pi_2}{C_2K_2} \quad \frac{\Pi}{CK} = \text{constant}$$

e.g. Calculate the mol. weight (M) of a substance when a solution containing 75 g dm^{-3} exerts a $\Pi = 4{\cdot}80$ atm at 10°C.

$\Pi_1 = 1$ atm — $\Pi_2 = 4{\cdot}80$

$K_1 = 273$ K — $K_2 = 283$ K

$C_1 = \frac{1}{22{\cdot}4}$ mol dm^{-3} — $C_2 = \frac{75}{M}$ mol dm^{-3}

$$\therefore M = \frac{75 \times 22{\cdot}4 \times 2{\cdot}83}{273 \times 4{\cdot}80} = 338$$

Isotonic Solutions Two solutions which have the same Π i.e. osmosis will not take place between them.

It can be seen that the laws of osmotic pressure are very similar to the gas laws. It can be assumed that the solute particles are behaving in the same way as the gas particles. The osmotic pressure is produced by the bombardment of the solution particles on the semi-permeable membrane, in the same way as the pressure of a gas is produced by the bombardment on the walls of the container.

For a Solution

$$\frac{\Pi}{CK} = \text{constant} \qquad C \propto \frac{1}{V} \qquad \therefore \frac{\Pi V}{K} = \text{constant}$$

which is equal to the gas constant R.

Measurement of osmotic pressure

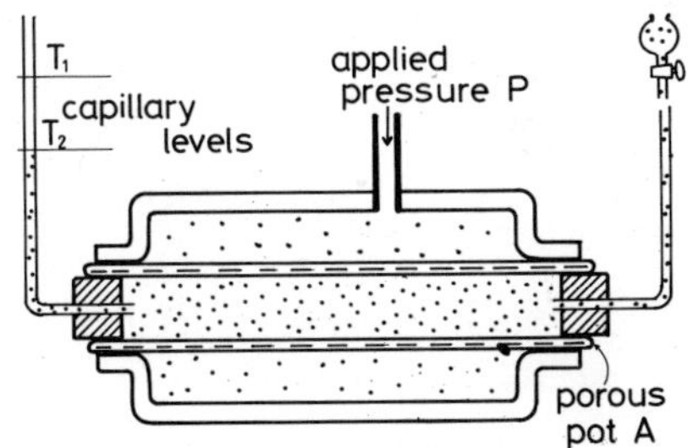

FIG. 9

The most efficient semi-permeable membrane is copper hexa cyano ferrate II which is strengthened by being formed in the walls of a porous pot *A*. Using the above apparatus the applied pressure P, which just prevents osmosis, is measured; this is Π. If P is greater than Π then T_1 and T_2 will rise, and if P is less than Π they fall. An average value of P when T_1 and T_2 are rising and falling slowly is taken.

N.B. (i) Π measurements are used for determining M of very large molecules, as the concentrations needed to obtain a measureable ΔT would be too large. As Π is generally large this does not apply.

(ii) Π is proportional to the rel. lowering of the vapour pressure and the limitations of Raoult's Law apply.

Comparison of $\Delta T_F + \Delta T_B$

Can be used for sugar urea etc.

For accuracy the solutions must be less than 0·1M.

(i) $\Delta T_F > \Delta T_B$ for solutions of same concentration.

(ii) ΔT_F is not affected appreciably by changes in atmospheric pressure, ΔT_B is $\therefore \Delta T_F$ is more accurate but ΔT_B quicker.

Abnormal molecular weights

In Solution The colligative properties ΔT_F, ΔT_B, and Π depend on the number of particles present in a given volume and not upon their nature, $\therefore$ on dissociation each ion formed will have the same effect as 1 mole of the undissociated electrolyte, i.e. will produce abnormally small molecular weights. Similarly association will give abnormally high molecular weights.

Van't Hoff Factor (i)

$$i = \frac{\text{observed coll. property}}{\text{calculated coll. property}}$$

Consider 1 mole of electrolyte A which dissociates into n ions, with degree of dissociation α. The total number of moles of A and moles of ions in soln. $= (1-\alpha) + n\alpha$

$$\therefore i = \frac{1-\alpha+n\alpha}{1} \qquad \alpha = \frac{i-1}{n-1}$$

N.B. $i = \dfrac{\text{calculated M}}{\text{observed M}}$

Thermal Dissociation

Dissociation often occurs on heating above the boiling point and is shown by a decrease in vapour density.

Example: The vapour density of phosphorous $\underline{V}$ chloride at 200 C and atmospheric pressure is 70 25. Calculate the degree of dissociation.

Let the degree of dissociation be a and consider 1 mole PCl_5

$$PCl_5 \rightleftharpoons PCl_3 + Cl_2$$

at equilibrium $1-a$ a   a moles

Total number of moles $= (1-a+2a) = (1+a)$.

If there had been no dissociation, only 1 mole PCl_5 present

$$\frac{\text{vol. of vapour as a result of dissociation}}{\text{vol. of vapour if no dissociation}} = \frac{1+a}{1}$$

but increase in volume is inversely to V.D.

$$\frac{\text{V.D. as a result of dissociation}}{\text{V.D. if no dissociation}} = \frac{1}{1+a}$$

V.D. PCl_5 if no dissociation $= MW/2 = 104{\cdot}25$

$$\therefore \frac{70{\cdot}25}{104{\cdot}25} = \frac{1}{1+a} \qquad a = 0{\cdot}4841$$

Degree of dissociation is 0·4841.

Rate of reaction

SOME METHODS USED TO INVESTIGATE THE RATE OF A REACTION

The rate of a reaction can be followed by measuring some property associated with the reaction and which changes during the course of the reaction. The rate must be expressed as a quantity per unit time and it is the **average** rate for the time chosen.

1. **Measurement of gas evolved**
The gas evolved displaces water from a burette and the volume of gas displaced is noted every 10 seconds. By plotting a graph of volume against time, the rate at any particular time can be found by drawing a tangent to the curve and measuring its slope.

2. **Colorimetry**
If a reaction mixture is coloured initially but loses this colour as the reaction proceeds, the progress of the reaction can be followed by using a colorimeter.

3. **Measuring the optical activity of a solution**
e.g. sucrose is hydrolysed to glucose and fructose. Sucrose is dextrorotatory but fructose is strongly laevorotatory and this outweighs the effect of the weakly dextrorotatory glucose so that the products give a laevorotation. Hence, as the concentration of the products increases there is a change in rotation from + to −.

4. **Titrimetric**
One method is to quench the reaction mixture in some way and withdraw samples at intervals and titrate these with some standard reagent. Thus the rate of disappearance of a reactant or formation of a product can be followed.

RATE EQUATION

Rate expressions cannot be derived from stoichiometric equations but only from experimental results. In the iodination of acetone it can be shown that the rate of the reaction is proportional to (1) the concentration of acetone (2) the hydrogen ion concentration, but it is unaffected by $[I_2]$.

$\text{Rate} = k[\text{acetone}][H^+]$

Units of $k = dm^3\,mol^{-1}\,s^{-1}$. k is the rate constant.

Order of Reaction $A + B \rightleftharpoons C + D$

If it can be shown that the rate of reaction is proportional to the concentration of A and also of B, rate $= k[A][B]$.

The reaction is first order with respect to A and first order with respect to B but second order overall. A first order reaction is said to have a constant half life i.e. the time taken for the concentration to decrease by one half is always the same and is independent of the initial concentration. This is not so for a second order reaction.

Rate of Hydrolysis of bromoalkanes

These can be compared by dissolving 3 drops of each in 1 cm^3 of ethanol. 1 cm^3 of silver nitrate solution is then added to each and the mixture shaken. The time taken for a precipitate to appear gives a direct measure of ease of hydrolysis.

THEORIES OF REACTION KINETICS

1. Collision Theory

This theory assumes that reactant molecules must collide before a reaction can occur. The rate of reaction is usually less than the collision rate indicating that not all collisions result in reaction. It is only a fraction of all collisions which are effective and this can be expressed in the form of the Arrhenius equation $k = Ae^{-E/RT}$. k = rate constant, A is a constant known as the Arrhenius constant, E is the activation energy. Before molecules can react they must possess the necessary activation energy; the higher the temperature the greater the number of molecules which acquire the activation energy, and hence rate of reaction increases with temperature as indicated by the Arrhenius equation.

2. Transition State Theory

This theory assumes that collision occurs between reactant molecules resulting in the formation of an activated complex. This activated complex is of high energy and can decompose into the reactants or into the reaction products. Thus there is an equilibrium between the reactants and the activated complex and this equilibrium moves to the right as the activated complex decomposes to give products.

Equilibria

If a reversible reaction X=Y is carried out in a closed container, a point will be reached when the concentrations of X and Y are constant unless the conditions are changed. At this point, the system is said to be in equilibrium; this equilibrium is dynamic but since the rates of the forward and backward reactions are equal, the concentrations of reactants and products do not alter.

Equilibrium Law

For any reaction $aA + bB \rightleftharpoons cC + dD$

$$Kc = \frac{[C]^c[D]^d}{[A]^a[B]^b}$$

concentrations are expressed in moles.
This is often referred to as the Law of Mass Action.
If Kc is large there is a high proportion of products in the equilibrium mixture whereas if Kc is very small the proportion of reactants is large. Kc varies with temperature.

Some Important Reversible Reactions

(i) Esterification (liquid phase).
e.g. $CH_3COOH + C_2H_5OH \rightleftharpoons CH_3CO.OC_2H_5 + H_2O$
Let *a* moles of alcohol react with *b* moles of the acid to give *c* moles of ester at equilibrium in $V\,dm^3$.
Concentration at eqm.:

$$C_2H_5OH = \frac{(b-c)}{V}\,mol\,dm^{-3}, \qquad CH_3COOH = \frac{(a-c)}{v}\,mol\,dm^{-3}$$

$$CH_3COOC_2H_5 = [H_2O] = \frac{C}{V}\,mol\,dm^{-3}$$

$$K = \frac{c^2}{(a-c)(b-c)}$$

N.B. In this case K is independent of pressure.

(ii) **Reactants and Products Gaseous**
e.g. (i) $H_2(g) + I_2(g) \rightleftharpoons 2HI(g)$
Let *a* moles of H_2 react with *b* moles of I_2 to form $2c$ moles of HI at equilibrium in $V\,dm^3$.

$$K = \frac{[HI]^2}{[H_2][I_2]} = \frac{4c^2}{(a-c)(b-c)}$$

N.B. In this case K is independent of P. There is no change in volume during the reaction.

(ii) $PCl_5(g) \rightleftharpoons PCl_3(g) + Cl_2(g)$

Let a moles of PCl_5 dissociate to form b moles of PCl_3 and b moles at equilibrium with a volume of V dm³

$$K = \frac{b^2}{(a-b)V}$$

N.B. In this case K depends on P and T.

(iii) **Heterogeneous Systems**

$CaCO_3(s) \rightleftharpoons CaO(s) + CO_2(g)$

For gases a measure of concentration is the partial pressure, which when used produces an equilibrium constant Kp which is proportional to Kc. The Equilibrium Law does not apply to heterogeneous systems but as all solids exert a vapour pressure one can assume that the reaction is taking place in the vapour phase, i.e. homogeneous:

$$Kp = \frac{p_{CaO} \times p_{CO_2}}{p_{CaCO_3}}$$

and as V.P. of solid is a constant at constant temp.

p_{CO_2} = Constant. The **Dissociation Pressure.**

DISTRIBUTION OF A SOLUTE BETWEEN TWO IMMISCIBLE SOLVENTS

When a solute is shaken with two immiscible liquids, it distributes itself between them so that the concentration in one solvent is directly proportional to the concentration in the other.

$$\frac{\text{concentration of solute in liquid A}}{\text{concentration of solute in liquid B}} = \text{constant}$$

K is known as the distribution coefficient or partition coefficient and varies with temperature.

EQUILIBRIUM CONSTANT IN TERMS OF PARTIAL PRESSURE

In a mixture of gases, the partial pressure of each gas is proportional to the number of moles of the gas in the mixture. Consider the reaction $PCl_5 \rightleftharpoons PCl_3 + Cl_2$ at a total pressure of P atm.

Let initial $[PCl_5] = 1$ mole and the degree of dissociation is α

At equilibrium $[PCl_5]=(1-\alpha)$; $[PCl_3]=\alpha$; $[Cl_2]=\alpha$
Total no: moles at equilibrium $=(1-\alpha)+\alpha+\alpha=1+\alpha$

$$p_{PCl_5}=\frac{1-\alpha}{1+\alpha}\cdot P;\quad p_{Cl_2}=\frac{\alpha}{1+\alpha}\cdot P;\quad p_{PCl_3}=\frac{\alpha}{1+\alpha}\cdot P$$

Concentration of a gas is $\propto$ partial pressure of the gas

$$\therefore K_p=\frac{p_{PCl_3}\times p_{Cl_2}}{p_{PCl_5}}$$

$$K_p=\frac{\left(\frac{\alpha}{1+\alpha}\cdot P\right)\left(\frac{\alpha}{1+\alpha}\cdot P\right)}{\left(\frac{1-\alpha}{1+\alpha}\cdot P\right)}$$

$$=\frac{\alpha^2.P}{(1+\alpha)(1-\alpha)}$$

$$=\frac{\alpha^2.P}{(1-\alpha)^2}$$

Remember that in general terms for a reaction

$xA(g)+yB(g)\rightleftharpoons zC(g)$

$$K_p=\frac{p_C{}^z}{p_A{}^x\cdot p_B{}^y}$$

CHANGING THE CONDITIONS ON AN EQUILIBRIUM MIXTURE

This can be predicted using Le Chatelier's Principle which states that if a change is applied to a system in equilibrium, the equilibrium readjusts itself to reduce the effect of the change.

(i) **Adding or removing a substance** $A+B\rightleftharpoons C+D$. If A or B is increased, the equilibrium is displaced to the right producing an increase in [C] and [D]. If D or C is removed, the equilibrium moves in the same way.
(ii) **Temperature** Increase in temperature increases the rate of a reaction and displaces the equilibrium to the left if the forward reaction is exothermic (i.e. K decreases) and to the right if the reaction is endothermic (K increases).
(iii) **Pressure** If the pressure is increased, the rate of the reaction is increased and the equilibrium is displaced in favour of the reaction resulting in a decrease in volume.
(iv) **Catalysts** These affect the rate of the reaction but have **no effect** on the composition of **equilibrium position.**

SOLUBILITY PRODUCT

The solubility product of a sparingly soluble electrolyte A_xB_y is the product of the concentration of the ions raised to the corresponding power.

$A_xB_y \rightleftharpoons xA + yB$
$K_{sp} = [A]^x[B]^y$

When the product of the ionic concentrations exceeds the solubility product, the electrolyte is precipitated.

Examples 1. At 20 C solubility of AgCl in water is 1·507 10^{-3} g dm^{-3}. Calculate the solubility product at this temperature.

$AgCl \rightleftharpoons Ag^+ + Cl^-$
1 1 1
mole mole mole

$$\text{No. of moles AgCl} = \frac{1{\cdot}507 \times 10^{-3}}{MW} = \frac{1{\cdot}507 \times 10^{-3}}{143{\cdot}5}$$

$$\therefore \text{No. of moles } Ag^+ = \frac{1{\cdot}507 \times 10^{-3}}{143{\cdot}5}$$

$$\text{No. of moles } Cl^- = \frac{1{\cdot}507 \times 10^{-3}}{143{\cdot}5}$$

$$K_{sp} = [Ag^+][Cl^-] = \left(\frac{1{\cdot}507 \times 10^{-3}}{143{\cdot}5}\right) \text{ mol}^2\text{ dm}^{-6}$$

$$\mathbf{K_{sp} = 1{\cdot}104 \times 10^{-10}\ mol^2\ dm^{-6}}$$

2. K_{sp} for copper II sulphide at 18 C is 1×10^{-40}. Find the solubility of copper II sulphide at this temperature.
$[Cu^{2+}][S^{2-}] = 1 \times 10^{-40}$
Now $CuS \rightleftharpoons Cu^{2+} + S^{2-}$
1 1 1
mole mole mole

Every mole of CuS which ionizes gives 1 mole Cu^{2+} and 1 mole S^{2-}, i.e. concentrations of Cu^{2+} and S^{2-} are equal.

$$[Cu^{2+}] = \sqrt{1 \times 10^{-40}}$$

$$\therefore \text{No. of moles CuS} = \sqrt{1 \times 10^{-40}}$$

$$\therefore \text{Solubility CuS} = \sqrt{1 \times 10^{-40}} \times MW$$

$$= \sqrt{1 \times 10^{-40}} \times 95{\cdot}5$$

$$\mathbf{= 9{\cdot}55 \times 10^{-21}\ g\ dm^{-3}}$$

Electrochemistry

CELLS

A Daniell cell consists of two half cells separated by a porous pot.
(i) zinc metal in zinc sulphate solution
(ii) copper metal in copper sulphate solution
Electrons are transferred from the zinc rod to the copper rod.
$Zn(s) \rightarrow Zn^{2+}(aq) + 2e \qquad Cu^{2+}(aq) + 2e \rightarrow Cu(s)$

Note the zinc has lost electrons and has been oxidized whereas the copper ions have gained electrons and been reduced.
If a valve voltmeter (high resistance) is put in the circuit, a P.D. of 1·1 V is observed, the copper plate being positive with respect to zinc.

This may be expressed as a **cell diagram**
$Zn(s) \mid Zn^{2+}(aq) \vdots Cu^{2+}(aq) \mid Cu(s) \qquad E = +1{\cdot}1\,V$
E represents the e.m.f. of the cell and the sign indicates the polarity of the right hand electrode in the diagram. To measure the e.m.f. of a cell a voltmeter of high resistance must be used so that the current taken will be very small. E varies with temperature and concentration of the ion, and hence the need for **Standard Electrode Potential** E^{θ}
This is the value of the electrode potential relative to the standard hydrogen electrode at a temperature of 298 K and an ion concentration of one mole per cubic decimetre. If two electrodes are joined to form a chemical cell and the standard electrode potential of each is known, the e.m.f. of the cell can be found. If standard conditions are not used, the cell e.m.f. will vary slightly.
e.g. find the e.m.f. of a cell containing the electrodes

$Pb(s) \mid Pb^{2+}(aq)$ and $Zn(s) \mid Zn^{2+}(aq)$

From data $Zn^{2+}(aq) \mid Zn(s); \quad E^{\theta} = -0{\cdot}76\,V$
$Pb^{2+}(aq) \mid Pb(s); \quad E^{\theta} = -0{\cdot}13\,V$

The cell diagram is $Zn(s) \mid Zn^{2+}(aq) \vdots Pb^{2+}(aq) \mid Pb(s)$

$$\underbrace{+0.76\,V \qquad\qquad -0.13\,V}_{+0.63\,V}$$

Note the sign of the E^θ value for the zinc electrode was reversed

$Zn(s) \mid Zn^{2+}(aq) \vdots Pb^{2+}(aq) \mid Pb(s) \qquad E^\theta = 0{\cdot}63\,V$

NERNST EQUATION

$$E = E^\theta + \frac{RT}{nF} \log_e \frac{[\text{oxidized form}]}{[\text{reduced form}]}$$

in a metal/metal ion system the metal is the reduced form and since it is a solid, its concentration is constant

∴ the Nernst equation can be rewritten

$$E = E^\theta + \frac{0{\cdot}059}{n} \log_{10} [\text{ion}] \qquad n = \text{charge on the ion.}$$

If E is determined at different ionic concentrations and E is plotted against $\log_{10}$ ion the slope of the line will be 0·059/n. From measurements of E, the concentration of ions in very dilute solutions can be found.

OSTWALD'S DILUTION LAW

Consider 1 mole of weak electrolyte AB dissociating in solution of V cubic decimetres with degree of dissociation α

$AB \rightleftharpoons A^+ + B^-$

at equilibrium $[AB] = \frac{1-\alpha}{V}, \quad [A^+] = \frac{\alpha}{V}, \quad [B^-] = \frac{\alpha}{V}$

Applying Equilibrium Law:

$$K = \frac{\alpha^2}{(1-\alpha)\,V} = \text{Dissociation Constant}$$

If K is calculated for strong electrolytes it is found that it varies considerably at different dilutions, but for weak electrolytes there is good agreement. For weak electrolytes $(1-\alpha)$ is approximately 1.

$$\therefore K = \frac{\alpha^2}{V} \quad \text{or} \quad \alpha = \sqrt{KV}$$

Acids and Bases A strong acid readily loses a proton and is highly dissociated in solution, a weak acid loses a proton with difficulty and is slightly dissociated.

Bases A strong base readily accepts a proton and is highly ionised, weak base accepts a proton with difficulty and is slightly dissociated.

The dissociation of water Very pure water has a small conductivity due to dissociation.

$2H_2O \rightleftharpoons H_3O^+ + OH^-$, $[H_2O \rightleftharpoons H^+ + OH^-]$

By the **Equilibrium Law** $\mathbf{K} = \frac{[H^+][OH^-]}{[H_2O]}$

because the dissociation is small $[H_2O]$ = constant at constant temperature.

$\therefore [H^+][OH^-]$ = constant = K_W – the **Ionic Product of water** = $\mathbf{10^{-14}}$ **at 25°C.**

Varies with temperature.

MEASUREMENT OF $[H^+(aq)]$

The hydrogen ion concentration is related directly to the pH value of the solution which can be measured directly using a pH meter.

$\mathbf{pH = -\log_{10}[H^+]}$

The concentration of hydrogen ion is measured in mol dm^{-3}.

E.g. the pH of 0·01 M acetic acid is 3·38. Find the $[H^+]$.

$$pH = -\log_{10}[H^+] = 3{\cdot}38$$
$$\text{or } \log_{10}[H^+] = -3{\cdot}38 = \bar{4}{\cdot}62$$
$$\text{Antilog } \bar{4}{\cdot}62 = 0{\cdot}0004169$$
$$[H^+] = 4{\cdot}169 \times 10^{-4} \text{ mol dm}^{-3}$$

Calculation of dissociation constant

$HA \rightleftharpoons H^+ + A^-$

For a weak acid HA, $K_a = \frac{[H^+][A^-]}{[HA]}$

K_a is the dissociation constant.

e.g. $[H^+]$ of 0·01 M solution of acetic acid is $4{\cdot}169 \times 10^{-4}$ mol dm^{-3}. Calculate K_a for acetic acid.

Method (i) making use of Ostwald's dilution law

$[H^+] = \sqrt{K/V}$

$$\therefore K = [H^+]^2 \times V \qquad V = 10^2$$
$$= (4{\cdot}169 \times 10^{-4})^2 \times 10^2$$
$$= \mathbf{1{\cdot}738 \times 10^{-5} \text{ mol dm}^{-3}}$$

Method (ii) $CH_3COOH \rightleftharpoons CH_3COO^- + H^+$

at equilibrium (0·01 − a) a a mol dm^{-3}

$$\therefore Ka = \frac{a^2}{(0{\cdot}01 - a)}$$

The concentration of hydrogen ions from the ionization of water is ignored as this is small in comparison with that from the acid

$$Ka = \frac{(4{\cdot}169 \times 10^{-4})^2}{(0{\cdot}01 - 4{\cdot}169 \times 10^{-4})}$$

An approximation may be made $(0{\cdot}01 - a) \simeq 0{\cdot}01$

$$Ka = \left(\frac{4{\cdot}169 \times 10^{-4}}{0{\cdot}01}\right)^2$$

$$= \mathbf{1{\cdot}738 \times 10^{-5}\ mol\ dm^{-3}}$$

Calculation of pH from Dissociation Constant

If the dissociation constant of an acid is known, the pH of a solution of known molarity can be found. E.g. Ka for benzoic acid is $6{\cdot}60 \times 10^{-5}$. Calculate $[H^+]$ and pH of a 0·01 M solution of the acid.

Method (i) $[H^+] = \sqrt{\frac{K}{V}}$ 0·01 M = dilution of 100

$$= \sqrt{\frac{6{\cdot}60 \times 10^{-5}}{10^2}}$$

$$= 8{\cdot}123 \times 10^{-4}\ mol\ dm^{-3}$$

Method (ii) $C_6H_5COOH \rightleftharpoons C_6H_5COO^- + H^+$

0·01 − a a a

$$Ka = \frac{a^2}{(0{\cdot}01 - a)} \simeq \frac{a^2}{0{\cdot}01}$$

$$6{\cdot}60 \times 10^{-5} = \frac{a^2}{0{\cdot}01}$$

$$\therefore a = \sqrt{6{\cdot}60 \times 10^{-5} \times 0{\cdot}01}$$

$$a = [H^+] = \mathbf{8{\cdot}123 \times 10^{-4}\ mol\ dm^{-3}}$$

$$pH = -\log_{10}[H^+]$$

$$\log_{10}[H^+] = \log_{10} 8{\cdot}123 \times 10^{-4} = \bar{4}{\cdot}9097$$

$$= -4 + 0{\cdot}9097$$

$$= -3{\cdot}0903$$

$$-\log_{10}[H^+] = 3{\cdot}0903 \qquad \therefore \mathbf{pH = 3{\cdot}0903}$$

Buffer Solutions

The pH of a buffer solution is relatively unaffected by the addition of small quantities of acid or alkali.

Type 1 is made from a weak acid and its sodium salt e.g. acetic acid and sodium acetate

(a) $CH_3COOH \rightleftharpoons H^+ + CH_3COO^-$ slight dissociation

(b) $CH_3COONa \rightleftharpoons Na^+ + CH_3COO^-$ complete dissociation

When H^+ is added it is removed by combination with the acetate ion to form acetic acid. When OH^- is added it is removed by combination with H^+ to form H_2O and (a) is displaced to the right maintaining the H^+

Applying Eqm. Law to the acid $Ka = \frac{[H^+][CH_3COO^-]}{[CH_3COOH]}$

$$\therefore [H^+] = \frac{Ka[CH_3COOH]}{[CH_3COO^-]}$$

$[CH_3COO^-]$ from the acid is negligible compared with that from the salt

$$\therefore H^+ = \frac{K_a[\text{acid}]}{[\text{salt}]}$$

$$pH = -\log_{10}[H^+]$$

$$\therefore pH = -\log Ka - \log\left(\frac{[\text{acid}]}{[\text{salt}]}\right)$$

Note (i) the pH of a buffer solution is dependent on the **ratio** of the concentrations of acid and salt.

(ii) since the acetate ion is the corresponding **base** of acetic acid the expression may be written

$$pH = -\log Ka - \log\left(\frac{[\text{acid}]}{[\text{base}]}\right)$$

Type 2 is made from a weak base and a salt of the base e.g. a mixture of ammonium chloride (strongly ionized) and ammonia (very feebly ionized).

Indicators

The end point of an acid/alkali titration does not necessarily correspond to pH=7. The indicator used must be able to detect the pH of the solution at the end point.

An indicator is a weak acid or base in which the colour of the un-ionised substance is different from that of the ions.

General Points about Periodic Table

1. There is an **increase in electropositivity down a group** due to the increasing size of the atoms. The force holding the electrons in the outer shell becomes weaker as the distance becomes greater; this effect is enhanced by the screening effect of complete shells in the atom. This is shown by an increase in the metallic (basic) characteristics of the elements.

2. There is a **decrease in the electropositivity across the period** due to the increasing difficulty in losing larger numbers of electrons. This is shown by an increase in the non-metallic (acidic) properties, i.e. covalent bonds and negative ions are formed.

3. As a result of these two trends there are some considerable **diagonal similarities** between elements in different groups.

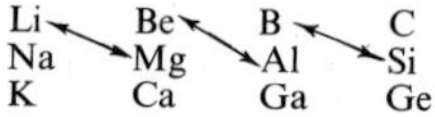

Li ↘	Be ↘	B ↘	C
Na	Mg	Al	Si
K	Ca	Ga	Ge

Li and Mg, Be and Al, B and Si.

As the chemical properties depend on the outer or valency electrons it is to be expected that elements in the same group will have similar properties.

4. **The position of hydrogen.**

H has only 1 electron and 1 proton, i.e. the only element which does not contain a neutron. It shows properties which are similar to Group 1 and Group 7 (Halogens).

Group 1. (i) 1 electron in outer shell, (ii) forms positive ions, H^+ in dil. acids as does Na^+, K^+ etc.

Group 7. (i) Physical state, (ii) forms negative ions H^- in hydrides NaH, CaH_2, etc. as does Cl^-, Br^-, etc., (iii) forms covalent bonds H—H, H—Cl, etc.

H is usually considered alone.

General Properties of Transition Elements.

1. Weakly electropositive.
2. Variable oxidation states.
3. coloured ions.
4. catalytic properties.

Oxidation Number

This is a useful concept in relation to the combining power of an element or ion and also to the classification of reactions as oxidations or reductions.

Rules for finding oxidation numbers

1. Atoms of elements are given an oxidation number zero.
2. Oxygen has an oxidation number of -2 except in peroxides where it is -1.
3. F, Cl, Br, I when present in halides have an oxidation number of -1.
4. Hydrogen always has an oxidation number of $+1$ except in ionic hydrides.
5. Na & K $= +1$; Mg & Ca $= +2$; Al $= +3$.
6. In any compound the sum of the oxidation numbers is zero.
7. In a compound of a metal and non-metal, the metal is given a positive oxidation number and the non-metal a negative number. In other cases rules 1–6 above must be applied. e.g. in SO_3 oxygen is always -2 therefore the total for oxygen is -6 and sulphur must be $+6$.

Examples

(a) Manganese in MnO_4^-

Oxygen is -2 therefore the total for oxygen is -8 but the ion has one negative charge therefore manganese must be $+7$

MnO_4^-

$+7-4x2$

-1

(b) Phosphorus in H_3PO_4

Each hydrogen atom has an oxidation number of $+1$ therefore the total is $+3$. Therefore the phosphate ion must be PO_4^{3-}.

Each oxygen atom has an oxidation number of -2 therefore the total for oxygen is -8. The ion has three negative charges therefore phosphorus must be in the oxidation state of $+3$

(c) K_2CrO_4

$+2+x-8$

$+2+x-8=0 \quad x=6$

therefore $Cr=+6$

(d) $NaNO_3$

$+1+x-6$

$+1+x-6=0 \quad x=+5$

therefore $N=+5$

Oxidation and Reduction

If an element increases its oxidation number during the course of a reaction it has been oxidized but if there has been a decrease in the oxidation number it has been reduced.

Group 1

Alkali Metals Li, Na, K, Rb, Cs.
Each element contains one electron in the outer shell $-\mathbf{s}^1$ and therefore form M^+ ions by electron loss. The compounds are invariably ionic with high melting points and boiling points etc. There is a general increase in electropositivity down the group (Fajans Rules), which is shown by an increase in reactivity, and an increase in the stability of compounds such as oxides, hydroxides and salts. Lithium is alone in exhibiting slight covalent properties.

Elements They cannot be extracted by the chemical reduction of their oxides because these compounds are too stable. They are produced by the electrolysis of their fused chlorides and hydroxides.

Properties They are all soft, white and good conductors of heat and electricity, they tarnish rapidly in air. Reactions with (i) **Air/Oxygen.** Li will melt when heated and eventually burns to form the monoxide and some lithium nitride.

$4Li + O_2 \rightarrow 2Li_2O$; $6Li + N_2 \rightarrow 2Li_3N$
Na and K burn when heated to form a mixture of sodium monoxide and peroxide and potassium peroxide:
$2Na + O_2 \rightarrow Na_2O_2$; $K + O_2 \rightarrow KO_2$;
Rb & Cs ignite spontaneously to form peroxides. In air all metals tarnish rapidly due to the formation of the carbonate, **(ii) with water they** all react readily to form the hydroxide and hydrogen:

$$2M + 2H_2O \rightarrow 2MOH + H_2$$

Lithium is comparatively slow whereas Cs is violent. The corresponding reactions with dilute acids are even more violent, **(iii) Hydrogen** reacts when heated to form hydrides.

$$2M + H_2 \rightarrow 2MH$$

(iv) Ammonia reacts to form amides

$$2M + 2NH_3 \rightarrow 2MNH_2 + H_2$$

COMPOUNDS

Oxides are prepared by direct combination, not by decomposition of hydroxides, nitrates, and carbonates. The monoxides are all strongly basic and react vigorously with water:

$M_2O + H_2O \rightarrow 2MOH$

Peroxides Also formed by direct combination. They are true peroxides, i.e. they react with cold dilute acids to liberate hydrogen peroxide.

$M_2O_2 + 2H^+ \rightarrow 2M^+ + H_2O_2$

Hydrides Made by direct combination. They are all salt like compounds which give hydrogen at the anode when electrolysed in the fused state (H^-). They are hydrolysed by water.

$MH + H_2O \rightarrow MOH + H_2$

The stability decreases down the group.

Hydroxides They are soluble and stable to heat. LiOH is the only one which is decomposed when heated. Compare with group 2.

Carbonates As above they are only soluble carbonates. Li_2CO_3 decomposes when heated and is only sparingly soluble, compare group 2.

$Li_2CO_3 \rightarrow Li_2O + CO_2$

Sulphides Prepared by direct combination and with H_2S and alkali. They are soluble in water and appreciably hydrolysed.

$M_2S + H_2O \rightarrow MHS + MOH$

They also form polysulphides:

M_2S, M_2S_3, M_2S_5, M_2S_6.

Nitrates Crystallised from neutral solution of base and nitric acid. They are the only ones which decompose on heating to give the nitrite:

$2MNO_3 \rightarrow 2MNO_2 + O_2$

Chlorides Prepared by the neutralisation of the alkali with dilute HCl. They are typical salts with the exception of LiCl which is deliquesent and partly hydrolysed, see group 2.

$LiCl + H_2O \rightarrow LiOH + HCl$

Flame colours Many elements give characteristic colours when their compounds are placed in a Bunsen burner flame.

Group 2

The Alkaline Earth Metals Be, Mg, Ca, Sr, Ba.

All contain 2 electrons in the outer shell $-\mathbf{s^2}$. They form M^{2+} ions losing these two electrons. They are not as electropositive as the corresponding Group 1 metals (Fajans Rules) and Beryllium shows considerable covalent tendencies. Group 1 and 2 elements are referred to as *s* block elements.

Elements Be and Mg can be extracted by electrolysis of fused chloride and by chemical reduction. Ca, Sr, Ba can only be extracted by electrolysis. Reactions with **(i) Air** All burn brilliantly when heated in air to form a mixture of oxide and nitride:

$$2M + O_2 \rightarrow 2MO; \qquad 3M + N_2 \rightarrow M_3N_2$$

the rate of reaction and the proportion of nitride formed increases down the group, **(ii) Water** Be does not react even when hot. Mg reacts very slowly with water but reacts readily with steam at red heat:

$$Mg + H_2O \rightarrow MgO + H_2$$

Ca, Sr, Ba all react readily with water:

$$Ca + 2H_2O \rightarrow Ca(OH)_2 + H_2$$

(The increase in the solubility of the hydroxide can account for part of the increase in vigour of the reaction). **(iii) Hydrogen.** Be and Mg, no reaction, others react on heating to form ionic hydrides similar to group 1.

$$Ca + H_2 \rightarrow CaH_2$$

(iv) **Oxygen** They all burn to form monoxides but Ca, Sr, Ba form stable peroxides also. (v) **Alkalis** Be dissolves to form beryllates which are similar to aluminates but less stable. The others do not react. (vi) **Acids** They react readily:

$$M + 2H^+ \rightarrow M^{2+} + H_2$$

Be rendered passive with nitric acid and Ba reacts slowly with sulphuric acid because it forms an insoluble sulphate.

COMPOUNDS

(i) **Oxides** All form basic oxides MO by heating the nitrate, carbonate, hydroxide or sulphate to constant weight. The solubility in water increases considerably down the group.

(ii) **Peroxides** Be not formed; Ca, Sr, Ba formed by direct combination with oxygen. All stable compounds which yield hydrogen peroxide with dilute acids.

$$BaO_2 + H_2SO_4 \rightarrow BaSO_4 + H_2O_2$$

(iii) **Hydroxides** Precipitated by the addition of alkali to corresponding metal ion in solution:

$$Mg^{2+} + 2OH^- \rightarrow Mg(OH)_2$$

the solubility and stability increase down the group:
$Ba(OH)_2$ quite soluble 4·2 g/100 g H_2O,
$Ca(OH)_2$ 0·01 g/100 g H_2O.
$Be(OH)_2$, $Mg(OH)_2$ decomposed by gentle heat. $Ca(OH)_2$, $Sr(OH)_2$ $Ba(OH)_2$ at red heat $M(OH)_2 \rightarrow MO + H_2O$. $Be(OH)_2$ is the only one which dissolves in alkalis the others are basic.

(iv) **Sulphides** Less soluble than alkali sulphides but still quite soluble. They can be made by direct combination. They are hydrolysed by water to give hydrosulphides:

$$2CaS + 2H_2O \rightarrow Ca(OH)_2 + Ca(HS)_2$$

Ca, Sr, Ba can form polysulphides (group 1 metals).

Hydrides Be and Mg hydrides cannot be formed directly but by reaction with lithium aluminium hydride on metal alkyl in ether:

$$LiAlH_4 + Be(CH_3)_2 \rightarrow LiAlH_2(CH_3)_2 + BeH_2$$

These are covalent. Ca, Sr, Ba formed by direct combination, these are ionic (as Group 1).

Chlorides $BeCl_2$ covalent, hydrolysed completely by water:

$$BeCl_2 + 2H_2O \rightarrow Be(OH)_2 + 2HCl$$

$MgCl_2$ more ionic though appreciably hydrolysed with boiling water. Ca, Sr, and Ba chlorides hydrolysed slightly. The anhydrous chlorides cannot be formed by heating the hydrates.

Carbonates On addition of Na_2CO_3 solution, carbonates are precipitated. Be, Mg form basic carbonates the others do not.
The stability increases down the group.

Nitrates Prepared in the usual way. They all decompose on heating to give the oxide, nitrogen dioxide and oxygen.
$2M(NO_3)_2 \rightarrow 2MO + 4NO_2 + O_2$

Group 3

B, Al, Ga, In, Tl.
They all have 3 outer electrons —**s^2p^1** and the main valency is 3 although monovalent compounds of thallium are stable.
Boron is the most electronegative element in group 3 and shows many properties which are not shared by other members of the group. Boron is a non-metal whilst the other elements are metals. Boron forms no simple ion and its compounds are covalent. Ionic and covalent compounds of aluminium exist and there is an increasing tendency down the group to form ionic compounds.
The hydroxide of boron is feebly acidic, aluminium and gallium hydroxides are amphoteric and the hydroxides of indium and thallium are basic.
Both boron and aluminium form compounds containing three planar covalent bonds. Since the boron and the aluminium atom can accept another pair of electrons, such compounds often combine with molecules having a lone pair of electrons e.g. $BF_3{\cdot}NH_3$

```
     F   H                    F   H
   ×·× ×· ×                   |   |
        ×                 F—B←N—H
 F ·B ×N ·H                   |   |
   ×·      ·×                 F   H
     F   H
```

The maximum covalency of boron is four but aluminium can show covalency of six e.g. $(Al(OH)_6)^{3-}$

ALUMINIUM $1s^22s^22p^63s^23p^1$

Extraction from bauxite $Al_2O_3.2H_2O$. This is heated with sodium hydroxide solution under pressure, the aluminium oxide dissolves and the impurities silica, iron oxides and titanium oxide filtered off. Aluminium hydroxide is then precipitated from the remaining solution of sodium aluminate by adding freshly precipitated aluminium hydroxide:

$AlO_2^- + 2H_2O \rightarrow Al(OH)_3 + OH^-$

The hydroxide is then heated to give pure molten aluminium oxide which is then electrolysed:

$2Al(OH)_3 \rightarrow Al_2O_3 + 3H_2O$

Aluminium oxide consists of Al^{3+} and O^{2-} ions. At the cathode $Al^{3+}+3e \rightarrow Al$; at the anode $2O^{2-}+4e \rightarrow O_2$, total reaction

$$4Al^{3+}+6O^{2-} \rightarrow 4Al+3O_2$$

Properties It forms a thin layer of aluminium oxide in air which protects aluminium from further attack because of the insolubility of this oxide in certain acids. Al does not react with nitric acid under any conditions nor with dilute sulphuric acid. However it will react with concentrated sulphuric acid to give aluminium sulphate and sulphur dioxide and with hydrochloric acid to give hydrogen and aluminium chloride:

$$2Al+6H_3O^{+} \rightarrow 2Al^{3+}+3H_2+6H_2O$$

Al will burn in air if heated to 1000°C to form aluminium oxide and nitride:

$$4Al+3O_2 \rightarrow 2Al_2O_3;\ 2Al+N_2 \rightarrow 2AlN$$

It reacts with sodium hydroxide solution to give sodium aluminate and hydrogen:

$$2Al+2OH^{-}+2H_2O \rightarrow 2AlO_2^{-}+3H_2$$

It will react with non-metals on heating:

$$2Al+3Cl_2 \rightarrow 2AlCl_3; \qquad 2Al+3S \rightarrow Al_2S_3$$

and at high temperatures will reduce the oxides of iron manganese and chromium. The thermite process makes use of these reactions e.g.:

$$Cr_2O_3+2Al \rightarrow Al_2O_3+2Cr$$

Aluminium Oxide Prepared by heating aluminium hydroxide:

$$2Al(OH)_3 \rightarrow Al_2O_3+3H_2O$$

It reacts with acids to form salts, and alkalis to form aluminates because in solution the equilibrium
$Al_2O_3+3H_2O \rightleftharpoons 2Al(OH)_3$
is set up (see below).

Aluminium Hydroxide
Prepared by adding aqueous ammonia to a solution of an aluminium salt:

$$Al^{3+}+3OH^{-} \rightarrow Al(OH)_3$$

In aqueous solution the ion $(Al(H_2O)_6)^{3+}$ is formed. This behaves as a weak acid i.e. proton donor.

$$(Al(H_2O)_6)^{3+} \rightleftharpoons H^{+}+\left(Al\begin{smallmatrix}(H_2O)_5\\ OH\end{smallmatrix}\right)^{2+}$$

Aluminium chloride

Prepared by heating aluminium in dry chlorine:

$$2Al + 3Cl_2 \rightarrow 2AlCl_3$$

It is hydrolysed by water evolving hydrogen chloride:

$$AlCl_3 + 3H_2O \rightarrow Al(OH)_3 + 3HCl$$

It sublimes on heating and between 190° and 350°C exists as Al_2Cl_6 molecules.

Alums

Alums are members of an isomorphous series.
Examination of the structure of crystals shows that the formation is best written as $M^1 M^3(SO_4)_2 12H_2O$.
M^1=monovalent metal M^3=trivalent metal
Potash alum $K\,Al(SO_4)_2 12H_2O$
Chrome alum $K\,Cr(SO_4)_2 12H_2O$
There are no alums containing lithium due to the small size of the lithium ion. If a crystal of potash alum is suspended in a saturated solution of chrome alum, the crystal continues to grow and becomes covered with a layer of chrome alum—this is called **overgrowth.**

Lithium Aluminium Hydride $LiAlH_4$

This is formed in solution when finely divided lithium hydride reacts with an ethereal solution of aluminium chloride.

$$4LiH + AlCl_3 \rightarrow LiAlH_4 + 3LiCl$$

It is a most useful reducing agent particularly because

$$\begin{matrix} \diagdown & & \diagup \\ & C{=}C & \\ \diagup & & \diagdown \end{matrix}$$

are unaffected and also carboxylic acids are reduced to the corresponding alcohols with a higher yield than can be obtained by other methods. Acid chlorides, esters, aldehydes and ketones are reduced to alcohols. Amides and cyanides are reduced to amines.
The reduction is carried out in ethereal solution.

Group 4

C, Si, Ge, Sn, Pb.
They all have 4 outer electrons $-\mathbf{s^2p^2}$ therefore all the elements form quadrivalent covalent compounds (non-metallic). Electrovalent compounds are formed by Sn and Pb but in this case the valency is 2, i.e. two outer electrons are inert. This tendency is more pronounced with Pb than Sn.

Stable Oxidation States

4	4	4(2)	4,2	(4)2
C	Si	Ge	Sn	Pb

There is a gradual increase in electropositivity down the group, with the result that at the extreme ends the elements appear to be quite different, e.g. carbon (non-metallic) and lead (metallic). On closer study it can be seen that this is in accord with the above mentioned trend.

ELEMENTS

C and Si are non-metals Ge—metalloid, Sn and Pb are metals although C and Si do conduct electricity to some extent (graphite). Reactions with (i) **Air/Oxygen**. With the exception of lead they all burn on heating to form the dioxide. Pb forms minium: $3Pb + 2O_2 \rightarrow Pb_3O_4$.
(ii) **Water** In general there is no reaction when cold but they all (except Sn and Pb) react with steam to form an oxide and hydrogen:

$C + H_2O \rightarrow CO + H_2$

$Si + 2H_2O \rightarrow SiO_2 + 2H_2$

$Ge + 2H_2O \rightarrow GeO_2 + 2H_2$

(iii) **Acids** Sn and Pb are the only ones which displace H_2. $Sn + 2H^+ \rightarrow Sn^{2+} + H_2$. They all react with hot conc. HNO_3, H_2SO_4, being oxidised in the process.
(iv) **Alkalis** With the exception of C and Pb they dissolve in a concentrated solution to form salts:

$Si + 2OH^- + H_2O \rightarrow SiO_3^{2-} + 2H_2$ silicates

$Ge + 2OH^- + H_2O \rightarrow GeO_3^{2-} + 2H_2$ metagermanates

$Sn + 2OH^- + H_2O \rightarrow SnO_3^{2-} + 2H_2$ stannates

COMPOUNDS

Oxides C and Si form acidic oxides (MO_2), but Sn and Pb form amphoteric oxides MO and dioxides MO_2.
Hydrides They all form covalent hydrides but the number formed diminishes considerably down the group as does stability. Decomposition Temperatures:

CH_4 800°C; SiH_4 450°C; GeH_4 285°C; SnH_4 150°C; PbH_4 0°C.

Chlorides They all form MCl_4 volatile liquids typically covalent. With the exception of C they are hydrolysed by H_2O:
$MCl_4 + 2H_2O \rightarrow 4HCl\uparrow + MO$

CCl_4 not hydrolysed since no *d* orbitals available for bonding. Sn + Pb form divalent ionic chlorides although $SnCl_2$ is considerably hydrolysed in water:

$SnCl_2 + H_2O \rightarrow Sn(OH)_2 + 2HCl\uparrow$($PbCl_2$ insoluble).

Hydroxides In the case of non-metals these appear as acids:
e.g. $C(OH)_4 - H_2O \rightarrow H_2CO_3$

carbonic acid, a weak acid which only exists in solution H_2SiO_3 silicic acid, weak acid generally considered to be hydrated silica. The salts, carbonates and silicates are invariably more stable.
$Sn(OH)_4$ precipitated by the addition of ammonia to tin IV chloride solution:

$Sn^{4+} + 4OH^- \rightarrow Sn(OH)_4$.

It dissolves in excess caustic alkalis to form stannates:

$Sn(OH)_4 + 2OH^- \rightarrow SnO_3^{2-} + 3H_2O$

$Pb(OH)_4$ does not exist. Sn and Pb form divalent amphoteric hydroxides $M(OH)_2$. They dissolve in excess to form -ites:

$Sn(OH)_2 + 2OH^- \rightarrow SnO_2^{2-} + 2H_2O$

$Pb(OH)_2 + 2OH^- \rightarrow PbO_2^{2-} + 2H_2O$

N.B. Tin IV compounds are more stable than tin II compounds, tin II salts are powerful reducing agents $Sn^4 + 2e \rightarrow Sn^{2+}$.
Similarly lead II compounds are more stable than lead IV compounds, lead IV compounds are oxidising agents:
(i) $Sn^{2+} + 2Hg^{2+} \rightarrow Sn^{4+} + Hg_2^{2+}$
(ii) $PbO_2 + 4HCl \rightarrow PbCl_2 + 2H_2O + Cl_2\uparrow$

Group 5

N, P, As, Sb, Bi.
They all have 5 outer electrons $-\mathbf{s^2p^3}$ and therefore the main group valency is 3 (covalent). With the exception of N the outer shells are able to take 10 electrons producing pentavalent compounds, but this is only pronounced with P, N and P form the M^3 ion by electron loss and Sb and Bi form the M^{3+} ion with two inert outer electrons (cf Sn and Pb).

Elements N and P are bad conductors of heat and electricity although the others, especially Bi, are quite good. N, P, As, Sb show allotropy. N and P are typical non-metals. As is metalloid and Sb and Bi metallic. Reactions with **(i) Air** N no reaction. P burns to form oxide; ($P_2O_3 + P_2O_5$), As and Sb when heated form M_2O but Bi only when heated strongly.

(ii) Water Bi is the only one which reacts being attacked by steam at red heat:

$$2Bi + 3H_2O \rightarrow Bi_2O_3 + 3H_2\uparrow$$

(iii) Acids None displaces H_2 but with concentrated HNO_3, P and As are oxidised to the ortho-ic acids H_3MO_4, Sb to Sb_2O_5 and Bi to $Bi(NO_3)_3$, the only metallic nitrate of the group.

$$Bi + 6HNO_3 \rightarrow Bi(NO_3)_3 + 3H_2O + 3NO_2\uparrow$$

Compounds

Oxides They all form $M_2O_5(M_4O_{10})$ and $(M_2O_3)M_4O_6$, although it is doubtful whether pure Bi_2O_5 has been prepared. M_2O_5 oxides are acidic: $M_2O_5 + 3H_2O \rightarrow 2H_3MO_4$.$N_2O_3$ and P_2O_3

are also acidic:

$$M_2O_3 + 3H_2O \rightarrow 2H_3MO_3.$$

As_2O_3 is amphoteric though predominantly acidic, dissolving in both acids and alkalis to form salts.

$$As_2O_3 + 6OH^- \rightarrow \underset{\text{arsenites}}{2AsO^{3-}} + 3H_2O$$

$$As_2O_3 + 6HCl \rightarrow 2AsCl_3 + 3H_2O$$

Sb_2O_3 is also amphoteric but with the basic properties stronger. It forms stable basic salts with the three mineral acids, but will also dissolve in caustic alkalis to form meta antimonites:

$$2OH^- + Sb_2O_3 \rightarrow 2SbO_2^- + H_2O$$

Bi_2O_3 is prepared by the decomposition of its nitrate (metallic) and is predominantly basic in forming the most stable salts of the group (even a basic carbonate), although it will dissolve in fused caustic soda to form metabismuthates in a plentiful supply of air:

$Bi_2O_3 + 2OH^- + O_2 \rightarrow 2BiO_3^- + H_2O$

Hydrides They all form covalent hydrides MH_3 which decrease in stability down the group. Decomposition temperatures:
NH_3, 1300°C; PH_3, 440°C; AsH_3, 230°C; SbH_3, 150°C; BiH_3, 26°C. NH_3 is a weak base, it forms stable NH_4^+ compounds, PH_3 can form PH_4^+ but the only stable salt is PH_4I—phosphonium iodide. The others cannot form MH_3 but when substituted with alkyl groups become stabilised, e.g. $As(CH_3)_4$ and $Sb(CH_3)_4$.

Chlorides MCl_3. N, P and As form covalent volatile liquids. Sb and Bi form white solids, they are all hydrolysed by water:

$NCl_3 + 3H_2O \rightarrow 3HClO + NH_3\uparrow$ (violently)

$PCl_3 + 3H_2O \rightarrow 3HCl\uparrow + H_3PO_3$

$2AsCl_3 + 3H_2O$ (excess)$\rightarrow As_2O_3 + 6HCl\uparrow$

Sb + Bi, $MCl_3 + H_2O \rightleftharpoons MOCl + 2HCl\uparrow$

Hydroxides (Oxyacids) all form $M(OH)_3$ but only $Bi(OH)_3$ is a base:
$Bi(OH)_3 + 3HCl \rightarrow 3H_2O + BiCl_3$

The others are acids H_3MO_3.

Formation of M^{3-} ion This can only occur with N and P. N combines with metals at red heat to form nitrides, e.g. Mg_3N_2, Ca_3N_2, AlN, Li_3N, which are hydrolysed by warm water:

$Mg_3N_2 + 6H_2O \rightarrow 3Mg(OH)_2 + 2NH_3\uparrow$

There are fewer phosphides and they are much less stable, e.g. Na_3P, Ca_3P_2 these are decomposed vigorously with water to form phosphine.

$Na_3P + 3H_2O \rightarrow 3NaOH + PH_3\uparrow$

Group 6

O, S, Se, Te, Po. – s^2p^6
These elements exhibit allotropy. They are electronegative forming divalent ions. The oxides of sulphur are acidic, those of tellurium are amphoteric and polonium shows some metallic character. Oxygen and sulphur are usually considered in more detail.

Unusual properties of water

1. B.P. of water much higher than expected – H_2O is a liquid whereas other group VI hydrides are gases.
2. Maximum density 4°C.
3. High surface tension.
4. High dielectric constant (relative permittivity which makes water a good solvent for some compounds).

Hydrogen Peroxide

Prepared by treating barium peroxide with dilute sulphuric acid:

$$BaO_2 + H_2SO_4 \rightarrow H_2O_2 + BaSO_4\downarrow$$

The dilute solution is concentrated by distillation under vacuum. H_2O_2 is a colourless liquid which decomposes rapidly.

$$2H_2O_2 \rightarrow 2H_2O + O_2$$

It is an excellent oxidising agent, e.g. it will oxidise acidified iron II compounds to iron III, nitrous acid to nitric, acidified potassium iodide to iodine:

$$2Fe^{2+} + 2H^+ + H_2O_2 \rightarrow 2Fe^{3+} + 2H_2O$$

$$NO_2^- + H_2O_2 \rightarrow NO_3^- + H_2O$$

$$2H^+ + 2I^- + H_2O_2 \rightarrow I_2 + 2H_2O$$

H_2O_2 can also react as a reducing agent in the presence of strong oxidising agents, e.g. it will reduce silver oxide to silver, acidified potassium permanganate solution to a manganese II salt:

$$Ag_2O + H_2O_2 \rightarrow 2Ag + H_2O + O_2\uparrow$$

$$6H^+ + 2MnO_4^- + 5H_2O_2 \rightarrow 2Mn^{2+} + 8H_2O + 50_2\uparrow$$

H_2O_2 also acts as a very weak acid:

$$H_2O_2 + H_2O \rightleftharpoons 2H_3O^+ + O^{2-}$$

and will form peroxides with bases:
$$BaO + H_2O_2 \rightarrow BaO_2 + H_2O$$

SULPHUR

Sulphur can have oxidation numbers from -2 to $+7$.

$+7$	$S_2O_8^{2-}$	persulphate
$+6$	SO_4^{2-}	sulphate. SO_3 sulphur trioxide
$+5$	$S_2O_6^{2-}$	diothionate
$+4$	SO_3^{2-}	sulphite, SO_2 sulphur dioxide
$+3$		
$+2$	$S_2O_3^{2-}$	thiosulphate
0	S_8	sulphur
-2	S^{2-}	sulphide

The possibility of converting sulphur from one oxidation state to another may be calculated from E^θ values see method page 56.

Sodium thiosulphate $Na_2S_2O_3 \cdot 5H_2O$
This is prepared by boiling sodium sulphite with sulphur

$$Na_2SO_3 + S \rightarrow Na_2S_2O_3$$

Sodium thiosulphate is a reducing agent and is used to estimate iodine, sodium tetrathionate being formed:

$$2S_2O_3^{2-} + I_2 \rightarrow 2I^- + S_4O_6^{2-}$$

The oxidation state of sulphur has changed from $+2$ to $+2\frac{1}{2}$ and hence the sulphur has been oxidised. The iodine has changed from 0 to -1 and has therefore been reduced. In acid solution, sodium thiosulphate disproportionates i.e. two different oxidation stated are formed.

$$\underset{+2}{S_2O_3^{2-}} + 2H^+ \rightarrow \underset{+4}{SO_2} + \underset{0}{S} + HO$$

Disproportionation does not occur in alkaline solution.

Hydrogen Sulphide Prepared by adding cold dilute hydrochloric acid to iron II sulphide.

$$FeS + 2HCl \rightarrow H_2S + FeCl_2$$

H_2S is a colourless poisonous gas smelling of 'bad eggs'. It is fairly soluble in water. H_2S normally burns to form water and sulphur:

$2H_2S + O_2 \rightarrow 2H_2O + S\downarrow$

but, with an excess of air, water and sulphur dioxide are formed

$2H_2S + 3O_2 \rightarrow 2H_2O + 2SO_2\uparrow$

H_2S acts as a weak dibasic acid in water:

$H_2S + H_2O \rightleftharpoons H_3O^+ + HS^-$
$H_2S + 2H_2O \rightleftharpoons 2H_3O^+ + S^{2-}$

and forms normal and acid salts e.g. sodium sulphide Na_2S, sodium hydrogen sulphide NaHS. H_2S is a very strong reducing agent e.g. iron III salts are reduced to iron II, acidified potassium dichromate to a green chromium III salt, acidified potassium permanganate to a colourless manganese II salt, and all amorphous sulphur is precipitated in each case

$2Fe^{3+} + S^{2} \rightarrow 2Fe^{2+} + S\downarrow$

$14H^+ + Cr_2O_7^{2-} + 3S^{2-} \rightarrow 2Cr^{3+} + 7H_2O + 3S\downarrow$

$16H^+ + 2MnO_4^- + 5S^{2-} \rightarrow 2Mn^{2+} + 8H_2O + 5S\downarrow$

H_2S will also precipitate sulphides of metals from solution of their salts e.g. $Pb^{2+} + S^{2-} \rightarrow PbS\downarrow$

Sulphur Dioxide Prepared by heating copper with concentrated sulphuric acid:

$Cu + 2H_2SO_4 \rightarrow CuSO_4 + 2H_2O + SO_2\uparrow$

SO_2 is a colourless heavy gas with an acid smell, highly soluble in water forming sulphurous acid:

$SO_2 + H_2O \rightleftharpoons H_2SO_3$

The acid cannot be isolated but its salts are well known.
H_2SO_3 forms normal and acid salts e.g. Na_2SO_3 sodium sulphite $NaHSO_3$ sodium hydrogen sulphite.
SO_2 is a reducing agent, reducing iron III salts to iron II, acidified potassium permanganate to colourless manganese II salts, acidified potassium dichromate to green chromium III salts. SO_2 in a few reactions can also act as an oxidising agent e.g. with burning magnesium.

Sulphuric acid

$2SO_2 + O_2 \rightleftharpoons 2SO_3 \ \Delta H = -197kJ$

Since the forward reaction is accompanied by a decrease in volume, theoretically $[SO_3]$ increased at high pressure. In practice this is uneconomic and a pressure of one atmosphere is used. As the reaction is exothermic, more sulphur trioxide is produced if the temperature is kept low. In fact a temperature of 450°C is used as this enables equilibrium to be attained more quickly. A catalyst is also employed to speed up the rate at which the equilibrium is reached, though it does not increase the yield of sulphur trioxide.
Prepared industrially by the **Contact process**.
(i) burning sulphur in air to form sulphur dioxide, or roasting a sulphide ore$\rightarrow SO_2$ or from anhydrite.
(ii) catalytically oxidising the SO_2 to form sulphur trioxide using vanadium pentoxide.
(iii) absorbing the SO_3 in cold concentrated sulphuric acid to form oleum:

$H_2SO_4 + SO_3 \rightarrow H_2S_2O_7$

(iv) converting the $H_2S_2O_7$ to the acid by dilution with water:

$H_2S_2O_7 + H_2O \rightarrow 2H_2SO_4$

Reactions
1. As a strong acid:

$H_2SO_4 + H_2O \rightleftharpoons 2H_3O^+ + SO_4^{2-}$

2. As an oxidising agent when hot and concentrated e.g. with metals and non-metals:

$Zn + 2H_2SO_4 \rightarrow ZnSO_4 + 2H_2O + SO_2\uparrow$

$C + 2H_2SO_4 \rightarrow CO_2\uparrow + 2SO_2\uparrow + 2H_2O$

3. As a non-volatile acid to displace more volatile acids from their salts:

$NaCl + H_2SO_4 \rightarrow NaHSO_4 + HCl\uparrow$

$KNO_3 + H_2SO_4 \rightarrow KHSO_4 + HNO_3$

N.B. Not for HBr and HI since these are both recucing agents.

4. As a dehydrating agent when concentrated, e.g. oxalic acid dehydrated to carbon monoxide and dioxide, formic acid to carbon monoxide, blue copper sulphate crystals to the white anhydrous salt, and sugar to carbon.

Group 7

Halogens F, Cl, Br, I, $-s^2p^5$
They contain 7 outer electrons and therefore form X^- ions by gaining one electron. They also exhibit single covalent and co-ordinate bonds by donating lone pairs, e.g. chlorates and hypochlorites. There is a gradual decrease in electronegativity down the group with I showing some metallic properties, e.g. in the formation of salts such as ICI_3 which conducts electricity in the fused state. Fluorine due to its small size and high electronegativity is somewhat different.

Elements
They are all coloured, with a gradual increase in melting pt. and boiling pt. down the group. F and Cl are both yellow-green gases, Br a red liquid and I a black crystalline solid with a metallic lustre. They do not react with oxygen.
Reactions with: **(i) Water** F reacts vigorously forming HF, O_2 and some ozone. Cl and Br dissolve, forming:

$X_2 + H_2O \rightleftharpoons HX + HXO$

hyp-ous acids which in sunlight decomposes:

$2HXO \rightleftharpoons 2HX + O_2$

I is insoluble and does not react. They dissolve readily in the presence of X^- due to the formation of $X_3{}^-$.

(ii) With hydrogen They all react: $H_2 + F_2 \rightarrow H_2F_2$ others $H_2 + X_2 \rightarrow 2HX$.

The vigour of the reaction decrease from F to I.F explosively, Cl explosively, in direct sunlight, Br slowly and I only when the vapour is passed over heated platinum. Because of this affinity for H they will react vigorously with compounds containing it, e.g. with warm turpentine

$C_{10}H_{16} + 8Cl_2 \rightarrow 1OC + 16HCl$

(iii) Metals F reacts with all metals (even gold and platinum at high temperatures) the highest oxidation state being formed. Cl, Br, and I react with most metals in a similar way.

(iv) As oxidising agents They all readily accept electrons.

$X_2 + 2e \rightarrow 2X^-$, the order of oxidising powers is: F, Cl, Br, I e.g.,

(a) with iron II salts:

$2Fe^{2+} + X_2 \rightarrow 2Fe^{3+} + 2X^-$

The halogens at the top of the group will displace those below from solutions of their salts e.g.

$Cl_2 + 2Br^- \rightarrow 2Cl^- + Br_2$

(b) Sodium Thiosulphate, Cl and Br, in solution will oxidise the thiosulphate ion to the sulphate ion with some sulphur precipitated:

$S_2O_3^{2-} + Cl_2 + H_2O \rightarrow SO_4^{2-} + 2Cl^- + 2H^+ + S$

but with the halogen in excess there is complete conversion to the sulphate:

$S_2O_3^{2-} + 4Cl_2 + 5H_2O \rightarrow 2SO_4^{2-} + 10H^+ + 8Cl^-$

I forms the tetrathionate ion:

$2S_2O_3^{2-} + I_2 \rightarrow S_4O_6^{2-} + 2I^-$

used in the quantitative estimation of I.

(v) Alkalis (a) when **cold and dilute** form -ide and hypo -ite:

$2OH^- + X_2 \rightarrow X^- + OX^-$

hypoiodite disproportionates (b) when **hot and concentrated** form -ide and -ates:

$6OH^- + 3X_2 \rightarrow 5X^- + XO_3^- + 3H_2O$

(c) with dry slaked lime Cl and Br form bleaching powders which liberate the halogen when acidified:

$Ca(OH)_2 + X_2 \rightarrow CaOX_2 + H_2O$

$CaOX_2 + 2H^+ \rightarrow Ca^{2+} + H_2O + X_2$

Halogen Hydrides All form covalent gaseous HX which ionise in water to form strong acids:

$HX + H_2O \rightleftharpoons H_3O^+ + X^-$

They are also reducing agents which on oxidation give the halogens e.g. with manganese dioxide:

$MnO_2 + 4HX \rightarrow MnX_2 + 2H_2O + X_2$

the reducing powers decrease from HI to HBr to HCl, this being an indication of the increase in electronegativity from I to Cl. HF is different in that it is a weak acid and reducing agent; this is due to the considerable hydrogen bonding which occurs in the molecule resulting in association.

Transition Elements

These are frequently referred to as d-block elements. A d-block element is one which forms some compounds in which the inner shell of d electrons is incomplete.

Sc	Ti	V	Cr	Mn
$3d^1 4s^2$	$3d^2 4s^2$	$3d^3 4s^2$	$3d^5 s^1$	$3d^5 s^2$
Fe	Co	Ni	Cu	Zn
$3d^6 4s^2$	$3d^7 4s^2$	$3d^8 4s^2$	$3d^{10} 4s^1$	$3d^{10} 4s^2$

1. VARIABLE OXIDATION NUMBER

Transition metals contain 3d and 4s electrons of comparable energy, and both can become involved in electron transfer.

e.g. **Vanadium** has oxidation numbers of **2**, 3, 4 and **5** (the most important are in bold) the electronic configurations are

Vanadium atom $3d^3 4s^2$;	V^{2+}	Ar ↑ ↑ ↑
Ar = Argon	V^{3+}	Ar ↑ ↑
$1s^2 2s^2 2p^6 3s^2 3p^6$	V^{4+}	Ar ↑
	V^{5+}	Ar

Manganese **2**, 3, **4**, 5, 6, **7**.

Manganese atom $3d^5 4s^2$	Mn^{2+}	Ar ↑ ↑ ↑ ↑ ↑
	Mn^{4+}	Ar ↑ ↑ ↑
	Mn^{7+}	Ar

Iron 2, 3, 6

Fe^{2+}	Ar ↑↓ ↑ ↑ ↑ ↑
Fe^{3+}	Ar ↑ ↑ ↑ ↑ ↑

Relatively stable oxidation states are observed when the d orbitals are empty ($3d^0$) and half full ($3d^5$).

Oxidation number charts can be drawn up.

e.g. for manganese			
	7	$KMnO_4$	MnO_3F
	6	K_2MnO_4	
	5		
	4	MnO_2	$MnCl_4$
	3		
	2	$MnSO_4$	$MnCl_2$
	1		
	0	Mn(s)	

Try to do this for some of the other d-block elements.

Redox potentials may be used to predict whether or not a reaction is likely to occur. The E^θ value must be known for each electrode system and if the overall E^θ is positive, then the reaction is likely to occur.
e.g. is a manganate likely to be made from a permanganate and manganese IV oxide in acid conditions?

E^θ values

(i) $2e + 2MnO_4^{-} \rightarrow 2MnO_4^{2-}$ $E^\theta = 0{\cdot}56\,v$
MnVII MnVI

(ii) $2e + 4H^{+} + MnO_4^{2-} \rightarrow MnO_2 + 2H_2O$ $E^\theta = +2{\cdot}26\,v$
MnVI MnIV

Problem: will MnVII + MnIV→MnVI?
Rewrite (ii) so that MnIV is on the L.H.S. This means $E^\theta = -2{\cdot}26\,v$
add (i) $2e + 2MnO_4^{2-} \rightarrow 2MnO_4^{2-}$ $E^\theta = +0{\cdot}56\,v$
to $MnO_2 + 2H_2O \rightarrow 2e + 4H^{+} + MnO_4^{2-}$ $E^\theta = -2{\cdot}26\,v$

$2e + MnO_2 + 2MnO_4^{-} + 2H_2O \rightarrow 2e + 4H^{+} + 3MnO_4^{2-}$ $E^\theta = -1{\cdot}70\,v$
or $MnO_2 + 2MnO_4^{-} + 2H_2O \rightarrow 4H^{+} + 3MnO_4^{2-}$ $E^\theta = -1{\cdot}70\,v$

Since the E^θ is negative, the reaction is not likely to proceed. In predicting whether or not a reaction will occur, it must be remembered that concentration or temperature change may affect the change although this is unlikely to do so if the E^θ value for the overall reaction is more than 0·4 v. E^θ values do not give any indication of how quickly a reaction will occur.

2. COLOURED IONS

Solutions of Fe^{2+} salts are green, Fe^{3+} yellow, Mn^{2+} pink, MnO_4^{-} purple, Cr^{3+} green, $Cr_2O_7^{2-}$ orange.
In fact these ions are usually liquids and it is not a simple Cu^{2+} ion which gives copper sulphate its characteristic blue colour but $(Cu(H_2O)_4)^{2+}$. It is more correct to say that transition metals give coloured compounds and frequently form complex ions which are coloured rather than to state that the transition metal ions are coloured.

3. PARAMAGNETISM

This arises from the presence of unpaired electrons which are found in many hydrated transition metal ions e.g. $(Fe(H_2O)_6)^{2+}$.

4. COMPLEX IONS

In a complex ion the central metal ion is surrounded by a number of other ions or molecules called **ligands**. Water is probably the most common ligand.

$Cu^{2+} + 4H_2O \rightleftharpoons Cu(H_2O)_4{}^{2+}$

If there are two ligands available then there are two competing equilibria. Blue ions of $(Cu(H_2O)_4)^{2+}$ are present in an aqueous solution of copper sulphate which forms some $CuCl_4{}^{2-}$ ions when concentrated hydrochloric acid is added. Addition of ammonia produces the royal blue tetraammine CuII ion $Cu(NH_3)_4{}^{2+}$.
If the stability constants are considered

$Cu(H_2O)_4{}^{2+} + 4Cl^-_{(aq)} \rightleftharpoons CuCl_4{}^{2-} + 4H_2O \ \log K = 5{\cdot}6$

$Cu(H_2O)_6{}^{2+} + 4NH_3 \rightleftharpoons Cu(NH_3)_4{}^{2+} + 4H_2O \ \log K = 13{\cdot}2$

it is seen that the $Cu(NH_3)_4{}^{2+}$ is more stable than the $CuCl_4{}^{2-}$ ion and hence the ammonia molecule competes more successfully for the Cu^{2+} than does the chloride ion.

Polydentate ligands

All the ligands met so far are monodentate i.e. they can only form one link with the metal ion. Bidentate ligands can form two links with the metal ion e.g. $NH_2CH_2CH_2H_2N$ (via the lone pair of electrons on each nitrogen atom) and E.D.T.A. ethylene diamine tetra-acetic acid is hexadentate.

HO_2CCH_2 CH_2CO_2H

$N{-}CH_2{-}CH_2{-}N$

HO_2CCH_2 CH_2CO_2H

The links form via the lone pairs of electrons of the two nitrogen atoms and of the singly bonded oxygen atom (part of the $-OH$) in each of the carboxyl groups.

Shapes of some complex ions

Where these are six ligands e.g. $(Cr(NH_3)_6)^{3+}$ the complex is octahedral. If three bidentate ligands replace these, then two optically active isomers are possible (each being the mirror image of the other). Where there are four ligands e.g. $(Cu(NH_3)_4)^{2+}$ the complex is usually planar.

5. CATALYTIC ACTIVITY

The metals catalyse gaseous reactions e.g. finely divided Fe in the formation of ammonia. The compounds are used for all kinds of reactions, e.g. MnO_2 in the decomposition of potassium chlorate, Cr_2O_3 in the combination of carbon monoxide and hydrogen to form methanol and Fe_2O_3 in the production of hydrogen from water gas. The catalyst enables the reaction to proceed by a path of lower activation energy.

IMPORTANT TRANSITION COMPOUNDS

Chromium III chloride

There are three forms:

A $(Cr(H_2O)_4Cl_2)^+Cl^-.2H_2O$ green
B $(Cr(H_2O)_5Cl)^{2+}2Cl^-.H_2O$ green
C $(Cr(H_2O)_6)^{3+}3Cl^-$ violet

If excess silver nitrate solution is added in turn to solutions of salts A, B and C, each solution containing one mole of the salt, only one mole of silver chloride is precipitated from A, two moles from B and three moles from C.

Sodium dichromate ($Na_2Cr_2O_7$) Orange-red crystalline solid prepared by acidifying sodium chromate solution with H_2SO_4:

$2CrO_4^{2-} + 2H^+ \rightarrow Cr_2O_7^{2-} + H_2O$

the Na_2SO_4 crystallises first and then the $Na_2Cr_2O_7$.

Potassium dichromate ($K_2Cr_2O_7$) Orange-red crystals made by mixing hot saturated solutions of KCl and $Na_2Cr_2O_7$. NaCl is precipitated and the $K_2Cr_2O_7$ crystallises on cooling.

Reactions (i) **With alkalis,** solutions are changed to chromates:

$Cr_2O_7^{2-}(\text{orange}) + 2OH^- \rightarrow 2CrO_4^{2-}(\text{yellow}) + H_2O$

(ii) **when heated** strongly decomposes to chromate, chromium III oxide and oxygen:

$4Cr_2O_7^{2-} \rightarrow 4CrO_4^{2-} + 2Cr_2O_3(\text{green}) + 3O_2$

$(NH_4)_2Cr_2O_7$ decomposes violently giving nitrogen. Once started the reaction spreads rapidly:

$(NH_4)_2Cr_2O_7 \rightarrow Cr_2O_3 + 4H_2O + N_2$

(iii) **as an oxidising agent**

Detection of Chromium Precipitated as green-grey hydroxide from solution with NH_4Cl and ammonia (Group 3). In the presence of H_2O_2 this dissolves in alkali forming yellow chromate solution:

$$2Cr^{3+} + 10OH^- + 3H_2O_2 \rightarrow 2CrO_4^{2-} + 8H_2O$$

This gives a yellow precipitate ($PbCrO_4$) with lead acetate solution.

Potassium Permanganate $KMnO_4$
Prepared by fusing KOH, $KClO_3$ in a nickel crucible with MnO_2:

$$2MnO_2 + 2OH^- + ClO_3^- \rightarrow 2MnO_4^- + H_2O + Cl^-$$

On extraction with hot water, a green solution is obtained due to the formation of some potassium manganate. This is removed by passing CO_2:

$$3MnO_4^{2-} + 4H^+ \rightarrow 2MnO_4^- + MnO_2 + 2H_2O$$

The solution is filtered through glass wool and crystallised. Powerful oxidising agent and when heated gives the manganate MnO_4^- and oxygen.

Potassium hexacyano-ferrate II
A yellow crystalline solid formed by adding $FeSO_4$ solution to KCN solution until slight precipitate is obtained:

$$Fe^{2+} + 6CN^- \rightarrow Fe(CN)_6^{4-}$$

The $K_4(Fe(CN)_6)$ is then crystallised.

Reactions (i) with iron II salts a white precipitate obtained, which is oxidised to Prussian blue on standing. (ii) with iron III salts dark Prussian blue obtained. $Fe_4(Fe(CN)_6)_3$ used as a test for Fe^{3+}. (iii) with copper II salts brown copper hexacyano-ferrate II is precipitated, used as a test for Cu^{2+} and as a semi-permeable membrane.

Potassium hexacyano-ferrate III $K_3(Fe(CN))_6$
Red crystalline solid made by oxidation of $K_4(Fe(CN)_6)$. With H_2O_2 in acid solution:

$$2Fe(CN)_6^{4-} + 2H^+ + H_2O_2 \rightarrow 2Fe(CN)_6^{3-} + 2H_2O$$

Reactions (i) with iron II salts blue precipitate. Turnbull's blue is formed. It is chemically the same as Prussian blue, used as a test for Fe^{2+}. (ii) with iron III salts gives a brown solution $Fe(Fe(CN)_6)$.

The Mole

One mole of any substance is the amount of substance which contains as many particles as there are atoms of ^{12}C in twelve grammes of ^{12}C. This number is very large and is the **Avogadro constant** $6{\cdot}02 \times 10^{23}$. In using the term mole it is necessary to specify what particles are referred to. One mole of hydrogen molecules is 2 g of hydrogen whereas one mole of hydrogen atoms is 1 g of hydrogen.
Concentrations of solutions are usually expressed as the number of moles of solute per cubic decimetre. A molar solution contains one mole of solute per cubic decimetre of solution. A solution may be molar with respect to one of the ions. e.g. A solution of calcium hydroxide containing $74\,g\,dm^{-3}$ is M with respect to calcium hydroxide but 2M with respect to the hydroxide ion.

VOLUMETRIC ANALYSIS

ACID-BASE REACTIONS

1. Solution D contains a mixture of sodium carbonate and sodium hydrogen carbonate.
$25{\cdot}00\,cm^3$ solution D required $12{\cdot}1\,cm^3$ of 0·109M hydrochloric acid using phenol phthalein as indicator. The resulting solution required a further $40{\cdot}1\,cm^3$ of 0·109M hydrochloric acid using methyl orange as indicator. Calculate the concentration of (i) Na_2CO_2 (ii) $NaHCO_3$ in $g\,dm^{-3}$ of solution D.

Principle

(i) using phenol phthalein, the end point is given when the carbonate is completely converted to hydrogen carbonate.

$CO_3^{2-} + H^+ \rightarrow HCO_3^-$

(ii) the end point with methyl orange as indicator indicates the completeness of the reaction of the hydrogen carbonate i.e. that originally in solution D+ that formed from the carbonate as in (i) above.

$HCO_3^- + H^+ \rightarrow H_2O + CO_2$

Calculation

(i) $12{\cdot}1\ \text{cm}^3$ $0{\cdot}109$M HCl contains $\frac{0{\cdot}109 \times 12{\cdot}1}{1000}$ moles HCl.

From (i) above, this HCl is reacting with $\frac{0{\cdot}109 \times 12{\cdot}1}{1000}$ moles CO_3^{2-} in $25\ \text{cm}^3$ solution D.

$\therefore$ in $1\ \text{dm}^3$ there are $\frac{0{\cdot}109 \times 12{\cdot}1}{1000} \times 40$ moles CO_3^{2-}

Conc. $Na_2CO_3 = \frac{0{\cdot}109 \times 12{\cdot}1 \times 40 \times 106}{1000}\ \text{g dm}^{-3} =$ **$5{\cdot}594\ \text{g dm}^{-3}$**

(ii) Now the $NaHCO_3$ produced from the Na_2CO_3 above would require a further $12{\cdot}1\ \text{cm}^3$ $0{\cdot}109$M HCl for complete reaction.
Therefore $(40{\cdot}10 - 12{\cdot}10) = 28{\cdot}00\ \text{cm}^3$ $0{\cdot}109$M HCl were used to react with the $NaHCO_3$ originally in $25\ \text{cm}^3$ solution D.

$28{\cdot}00\ \text{cm}^3$ $0{\cdot}109$M HCl contains $\frac{0{\cdot}109 \times 28}{1000}$ moles HCl

Now $H^+ + HCO_3^- \rightarrow H_2O + CO_2$

therefore this is reacting with $\frac{0{\cdot}109 \times 28}{1000}$ moles HCO_3^- in $25\ \text{cm}^3$ solution.

Therefore in $1\ \text{dm}^3$ there are $\frac{0{\cdot}109 \times 28 \times 40}{1000}$ moles HCO_3^-

Conc. $NaHCO_3 = \frac{0{\cdot}109 \times 28 \times 40 \times 84}{1000}\ \text{gdm}^{-3} =$ **$10{\cdot}26\ \text{g dm}^{-3}$**

2. $0{\cdot}25$ g of an impure sample of ammonium sulphate was boiled with $40\ \text{cm}^3$ of a solution of $0{\cdot}15$M caustic soda. After boiling the solution required $30{\cdot}12\ \text{cm}^3$ $0{\cdot}06$M sulphuric acid to neutralise the excess alkali. Calculate the percentage of ammonium sulphate in the sample.

Principle

(i) This is a back titration. H_2SO_4 is reacting with unused NaOH. Calculate the number of moles of excess NaOH.
(ii) Number of moles of NaOH originally added is known and therefore number of moles which reacted with the ammonium sulphate can be found by subtraction.
(iii) $NH_4^+ + OH^- \rightarrow NH_3 + H_2O$
$132\ \text{g}\ (NH_4)_2SO_4 \equiv 2$ moles NaOH.

Calculation

(i) $H_2SO_4 + 2NaOH \rightarrow Na_2SO_4 + 2H_2O$

$30{\cdot}12\,cm^3$ 0·06M H_2SO_4 contains $\frac{0{\cdot}06 \times 30{\cdot}12}{1000}$ moles

Since 1 mole H_2SO_4 reacts with 2 moles NaOH

$30{\cdot}12\,cm^3$ 0·06M H_2SO_4 is reacting with $\frac{2 \times 0{\cdot}06 \times 30{\cdot}12}{1000}$ moles NaOH = **0·0036 moles NaOH.**

(ii) Now $40\,cm^3$ 0·15M NaOH originally added and this contains $\frac{0{\cdot}15 \times 40}{1000}$ moles NaOH = 0·006 moles.

therefore (0·006 − 0·0036) moles NaOH reacted with the $(NH_4)_2SO_4$ i.e. 0·0024 moles NaOH used.

(iii) from equation 2 moles NaOH ≡ 132 g $(NH_4)_2SO_4$

therefore 0·0024 moles NaOH ≡ $\frac{132 \times 0{\cdot}0024}{2}$ g $(NH_4)_2SO_4$

$$\%(NH_4)_2SO_4 = \frac{132 \times 0{\cdot}0024 \times 100}{2 \times 0{\cdot}25} = \mathbf{63{\cdot}36\%}$$

REDOX REACTIONS

(a) Potassium permanganate

In acid solution $MnO_4^- + 8H^+ + 5e \rightarrow Mn^{2+} + 4H_2O$. This is a key equation. Another half equation should be written to represent the oxidation of the other reactant and then the stoichiometry of the reaction can be found.

1. A solution of ammonium oxalte was prepared by dissolving 1·502 g of the solid in water and making up the solution to $250\,cm^3$. $25\,cm^3$ of this solution just decolourised $21{\cdot}32\,cm^3$ of a solution of potassium permanganate. $25\,cm^3$ of solution X containing $29\,g\,dm^{-3}$ of a solid containing iron II sulphate just decolourised $24{\cdot}40\,cm^3$ of the same solution of potassium permanganate used above. Calculate the percentage of iron II sulphate in the solid used to make solution X.

Principle

(i) From the reaction with ammonium oxalte find the molarity of the $KMnO_4$ solution.

(ii) now find the number of moles of iron II sulphate and then concentration in $g\,dm^{-3}$.

(iii) calculate the percentage of iron II sulphate in the solid.

Calculation

(i) $C_2O_4^{2-} \rightarrow 2CO_2 + 2e$ (a)

$MnO_4^- + 8H^+ + 5e \rightarrow Mn^{2+} + 4H_2O$ (b)

Multiply equation (a) by 5 and (b) by 2 and then add

$5C_2O_4^{2-} + 2MnO_4^- + 16H^+ \rightarrow 10CO_2 + 2Mn^{2+} + 4H_2O$

Thus 5 moles $(NH_4)_2C_2O_4 \equiv 2$ moles $KMnO_4$

Given solution contains $\frac{1 \cdot 502}{124}$ moles $(NH_4)_2C_2O_4$ on 250 cm³ (MW = 124)

therefore there are $\frac{2 \times 1 \cdot 502}{5 \times 124}$ moles $KMnO_4$ in 213·2 cm³ $KMnO_4$

therefore in 1 dm^{-3} there are $\frac{2 \times 1 \cdot 502 \times 1000}{5 \times 124 \times 213 \cdot 2}$ moles $KMnO_4$

= **0·0228 moles.**

(ii) 25 cm³ solution X ≡ 24·40 cm³ 0·0228M $KMnO_4$

$Fe^{2+} \rightarrow Fe^{3+}$ multiply by 5 and then add to equation (b)

$MnO_4^- + 5Fe^{2+} + 8H^+ \rightarrow Mn^{2+} + 5Fe^{3+} + 4H_2O$

24·40 cm³ 0·0228M $KMnO_4$ contains $\frac{0 \cdot 0228 \times 24 \cdot 40}{1000}$ moles $KMnO_4$

Since $MnO_4^- \equiv 5Fe^{2+}$ this is reacting with 25 cm³ solution containing $\frac{0 \cdot 0228 \times 24 \cdot 40 \times 5}{1000}$ moles Fe^{2+}

therefore in 1 dm³ there are $\frac{0 \cdot 0228 \times 24 \cdot 40 \times 5 \times 40}{1000}$ moles Fe^{2+}

or $\frac{0 \cdot 0228 \times 24 \cdot 40 \times 5 \times 40 \times 152}{1000}$ g $FeSO_4$ (MW = 152)

$\% FeSO_4 = \frac{0 \cdot 0228 \times 24 \cdot 40 \times 5 \times 40 \times 152 \times 100}{1000 \times 29}$ = **56·99%**

2. 10 cm³ of a solution of hydrogen peroxide were diluted with water to 250 cm³. 25 cm³ of the diluted solution just decolourised 35·0 cm³ 0·02M potassium permanganate solution. Calculate the concentration in g dm^{-3} of the original hydrogen peroxide solution.

Principle

Calculate the number of moles of hydrogen peroxide in the diluted solution and hence in the original.

Calculation

$H_2O_2 \rightarrow 2H^+ + O_2 + 2e$ (a)
$MnO_4^- + 8H^+ + 5e \rightarrow Mn^{2+} + 4H_2O$ (b)
multiply (a) by 5 and (b) by 2 and add

$2MnO_4^- + 16H^+ + 5H_2O_2 \rightarrow 10H^+ + 5O_2 + 2Mn^{2+} + 8H_2O$
or $2MnO_4^- + 6H^+ + 5H_2O_2 \rightarrow 5O_2 + 2Mn^{2+} + 8H_2O$

35·0 cm³ 0·02M $KMnO_4$ contains $\frac{0{\cdot}02 \times 35}{1000}$ moles $KMnO_4$

Since $2MnO_4^- \equiv 5H_2O_2$
there are $\frac{0{\cdot}02 \times 35 \times 5}{1000 \times 2}$ moles H_2O_2 in 25 cm³ diluted solution
$= \frac{0{\cdot}02 \times 35 \times 5 \times 40}{1000 \times 2}$ moles dm^{-3} H_2O_2

Since original solution was diluted 25 times, original solution contains
$\frac{0{\cdot}02 \times 35 \times 5 \times 40 \times 25}{1000 \times 2}$ moles H_2O_2

or $\frac{0{\cdot}02 \times 35 \times 5 \times 40 \times 25 \times 34}{1000 \times 2}$ g dm^{-3} H_2O_2

= 59·5 g dm⁻³

(b) Iodimetry

250 cm³ of a solution C contains 0·892 g potassium iodate. 25 cm³ of this solution were measured out, excess potassium iodide added and the solution acidified. The liberated iodine was oxidised by 24·7 cm³ of a solution of hydrated sodium thiosulphate $Na_2S_2O_3{\cdot}5H_2O$. Calculate the concentration in g dm^{-3} of the sodium thiosulphate solution.

Principle

(i) Find the molarity of the potassium iodide solution.
(ii) Then find the molarity of the sodium thiosulphate solution.

Calculation

(i) $IO_3^- + 5I^- + 6H... \rightarrow 3I_2 + 3H_2O$
$I_2 + 2S_2O_3^{2-} \rightarrow 2I^- + S_4O_6^{2-}$
therefore $IO_3^- \equiv 3I_2 \equiv 6S_2O_3^{2-}$
Solution C contains 0·892 × 4 g dm^{-3} KIO_3
therefore molarity is $\frac{0{\cdot}89 \times 4}{214}$ (MW = 214)
= 0·017M.

25 cm³ 0·017M KIO_3 contains $\frac{0{\cdot}017\times 25}{1000}$ moles KIO_3
therefore since $IO_3^- \equiv 6S_2O_3^{2-}$ and 25 cm³ $KIO_3 \equiv 24{\cdot}7$ cm³ $Na_2S_2O_3$
there are $\frac{0{\cdot}017\times 25\times 6}{1000}$ moles sodium thiosulphate in 24·7 cm³ solution.
Therefore in 1 dm³ there are $\frac{0{\cdot}017\times 25\times 6\times 1000}{1000\times 24{\cdot}7}$ moles $Na_2S_2O_3$
therefore concentration is $\frac{0{\cdot}017\times 25\times 6\times 1000\times 248}{1000\times 24{\cdot}7}$
(M.W. $Na_2S_2O_3{\cdot}5H_2O = 248$)
$= \mathbf{25{\cdot}61\ g\ dm^{-3}}$

PRECIPITATION REACTIONS

1·814 g of a mixture of sodium and potassium chlorides were dissolved in water and the solution made up to 250 cm³. 25 cm³ of this solution required 25·05 cm³ 0·1M silver nitrate for complete precipitation of the chloride. Calculate the percentage of sodium chloride in the mixture.

Calculation

Let there be x g NaCl in the mixture
therefore there are $(1{\cdot}814-x)$ g KCl in the mixture
$Cl^- + Ag^+ \rightarrow AgCl\downarrow$
58·5 g NaCl ≡ 1 dm³M $AgNO_3$
74·5 g KCl ≡ 1 dm³M$AgNO_3$
therefore x g NaCl $\equiv \frac{x\times 10\,000}{58{\cdot}5}$ cm³ 0·1M $AgNO_3$
$(1{\cdot}814-x)$ g KCl $\equiv \frac{1000\times(1{\cdot}814-x)}{74{\cdot}5}$ cm³ M $AgNO_3$
$\equiv \frac{10000\times(1{\cdot}814-x)}{74{\cdot}5}$ cm³ 0·1M $AgNO_3$
but the mixture required 250·5 cm³ 0·1M $AgNO_3$
$$\frac{10\,000x}{58{\cdot}5}+\frac{10\,000(1{\cdot}814-x)}{74{\cdot}5} = 250{\cdot}5 \text{ cm}^3\ 0{\cdot}1AgNO_3$$
$$x = 0{\cdot}1875$$
% sodium chloride in the mixture $= \frac{0{\cdot}1875\times 100}{1{\cdot}814} = \mathbf{10{\cdot}34\%}$

Organic Chemistry

NOMENCLATURE

Difficulty is frequently experienced in naming compounds containing branched chains. Branched chains hydrocarbons are named by using a combination of the name of the alkyl groups and the name of the unbranched chain hydrocarbon. The hydrocarbon name is derived from the *longest* continuous carbon atom chain in the molecule.

$$\overset{5}{CH_3}\overset{4}{CH_2}\overset{3}{CH_2}\overset{2}{\underset{\large CH_3}{\underset{|}{C}}H}\overset{1}{CH_3} \text{ is 2-methyl pentane.}$$

The numbering used is such that the *lowest* number possible is used to indicate the position of the side chain.

In alkenes, the position of the double bond must be indicated and again, the lowest numbered carbon atom in the chain is used.

$CH_2{=}CHCH_2CH_3$	but-1-ene
$CH_3CH{=}CHCH_3$	but-2-ene
$CH_2{=}\underset{\large CH_3}{\underset{|}{C}}CH_2CH_2CH_3$	2-methyl penta-1-ene

Other examples may help to clarify this method of nomenclature.

$CH_3CH_2CH_2CH_2OH$	butan-1-ol
$CH_3CH_2CH(OH)CH_3$	butan-2-ol
$CH_3\underset{\large CH_3}{\underset{|}{C}}HCH_2OH$	2-methyl propan-1-ol

The names of functional groups must also be known e.g.:

Acid chloride	$CH_3CH_2CH_2COCl$	butanoyl chloride
acid amide	$CH_3CH_2CH_2CONH_2$	butanamide
carboxylic acid	$CH_3CH_2CH_2CH_2CH_2COOH$	hexanoic acid
ketone	CH_3COCH_3	propanone (acetone)
aldehyde	CH_3CHO	ethanal (acetaldehyde)

To write the structural formula for 1-bromo-3 methyl butan-2-ol, 'butan' indicates the largest chain of 4 carbon atoms C—C—C—C; a bromine atom must go on this first carbon atom, an –OH group on the second and a methyl radical on the third, and then add the hydrogen atoms.

$$C{-}\underset{\large CH_3}{\underset{|}{C}}{-}\underset{\large OH}{\underset{|}{C}}{-}C{-}Br$$

```
    H       H       H       H
    |       |       |       |
H—C———C———C———C—Br   or   CH3CHCH(OH)CH2Br
    |       |        \      |                |
    H      CH3       OH   H              CH3
```

1-bromo-3 methyl butan-2-ol

Diols e.g. $\overset{3}{CH_3}\overset{2}{C}H(OH)\overset{1}{C}H_2OH$ (i.e. CH_3CHCH_2OH with OH on carbon 2)

The carbon atom is numbered to show the position of the hydroxyl groups. The name is propane-1, 2-diol.
Note. (i) the lowest possible numbering is used.
(ii) it is propane -1-2-diol and not propane.
(iii) as always, hyphens are put on both sides of the numbers.

SUMMARIES OF REACTIONS OF PRINCIPAL CLASSES OF ORGANIC COMPOUNDS

It is only possible to cover some preparative methods and the main reactions in each case and these are usually given in general terms. At one time examination questions were always set concerning ethene or ethanol—the simpler members of the family being chosen. Now it is increasingly common to find examples of propene or butan-1-ol referred to in the question. Thus it is understood that the reactions are known in general terms and then the student should try to write equations for particular members of the homologous series. Another way to check if the reactions are known is to draw up a chart of the type shown for the alkenes, writing in appropriate reactions, conditions and products. If it is found that the reactions are not known, stop and learn them again before proceeding. Aliphatic and aromatic compounds are not considered separately but are discussed together according to the functional group. It should be remembered that side chain substitution products of the benzene ring generally behave similarly to the corresponding aliphatic compounds whereas nuclear substitution products (aryl compounds) usually have different properties.

Isomerism

STRUCTURAL ISOMERISM

This applies to two or more compounds having the same molecular formula but different structural formulae.

e.g.

```
    H   H   H   H                 H   H   H
    |   |   |   |                 |   |   |
H — C — C — C — C — H         H — C — C — C — H
    |   |   |   |                 |   |   |
    H   H   H   H                 H   |   H
                                  H — C — H
                                      |
                                      H
       butane                  2-methyl propane
```

```
    H   H                         H       H
    |   |                         |       |
H — C — C — OH                H — C — O — C — H
    |   |                         |       |
    H   H                         H       H
     ethanol                   di methyl ether
```

STEREOISOMERISM

This occurs when two compounds have the same molecular formula, the same structural formula but a different spatial arrangement of the atoms.

1. Geometrical Isomerism

This can only occur where there is no free rotation around two atoms.

e.g. in a

```
 \     /
  C = C
 /     \
```

```
X       Y             X       Y
 \     /               \     /
    C                     C
    ||                    ||
    C                     C
 /     \               /     \
X       Y             Y       X
```

Cis form **Trans form**

2. Optical Isomerism

Optical isomers are able to rotate the plane of polarized light in opposite directions, the one which rotates the plane to the right is **dextro rotatory** (d-form) and the one which rotates it to the left is **laevo rotatory** (l-form).

An equimolar mixture of the two does not rotate the plane and is optically inactive (dl-form).

Optically active substances contain an **asymmetric** carbon atom, which a carbon atom attached to four *different* groups.

Such a molecule has no plane of symmetry and can exist in two non-superimposable mirror-image forms. Example:

Lactic acid

$$\begin{array}{c} \mathrm{H} \\ | \\ \mathrm{CH_3{-}C{-}COOH} \\ | \\ \mathrm{OH} \end{array}$$

bromo propionic acid

$$\begin{array}{c} \mathrm{H} \\ | \\ \mathrm{CH{-}C{-}COOH} \\ | \\ \mathrm{Br} \end{array}$$

Note. When propionic acid is brominated the product will contain equimolar proportions of the d and the l form and will therefore be optically inactive. Such equimolar mixtures of optically active isomers are called racemates.

Resolution of racemates

1. Pasteur separated the two optically active forms of tartaric acid by preparing their sodium ammonium salts and crystallised the salts below 27°C when the two salts have distinct crystal shape and could be separated by **mechanical means**.

2. **Chemical methods** can be used and involve reacting the dl form with e.g. a l-base.

dl-acid + 2l-base→d-acid l-base + l-acid l-base + $2H_2O$

the two products are no longer optically active and may be separated by fractional crystallisation. The free acid is then liberated by hydrolysis. This method is also due to Pasteur as is the next.

3. **Biochemical method**

Bacteria sometimes feed in solutions of racemates and one form is consumed to the exclusion of the other. This method is wasteful and slow.

Organic Reactions

Mechanisms of reactions should be revised.

Bond fission

Chemical reactions may involve bond breaking and then the formation of new bonds. A covalent bond may be broken (i) so that each atom keeps one of the electrons forming the bond. $X\!:\!Y \rightarrow X\cdot + Y\cdot$.
This is called **Homolytic fission** or (ii) where one of the atoms retain both electrons $X\!:\!Y \rightarrow X\!:^- + Y^+$.
This is called **Heterolytic fission.**
If heterolytic fission occurs in a C—X bond it is the atom X which retains the electrons, then a positively charged carbonium ion is left. A carbonium ion is formed as an intermediate in many reactions e.g. when hydrogen halides react with alkenes e.g.

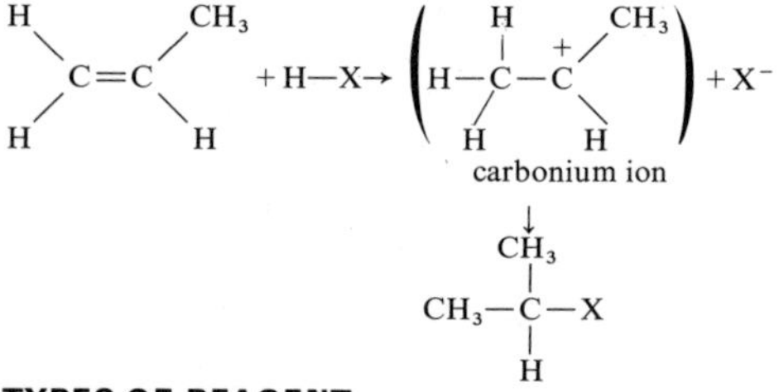

$$(H)_2C{=}C(CH_3)H + H{-}X \rightarrow \left(H{-}\overset{H}{\underset{H}{C}}{-}\overset{+}{C}(CH_3)H\right) + X^-$$

carbonium ion

$$\downarrow$$

$$CH_3{-}\overset{CH_3}{\underset{H}{C}}{-}X$$

TYPES OF REAGENT

Nucleophilic These reagents are either negative ions or possess lone pairs of electrons which they can donate to electron deficient atoms—examples: OH^-, Cl^-, Br^-, CN^-, H_2O, NH_3
Electrophilic These reagents are deficient in electrons and are often positive ions. They accept electron pairs. Example $NO_2{}^+$, H_3O^+, BF_3

Inductive Effect

Where there is an unequal sharing of a pair of electrons between two atoms, some polarity arises.

e.g. $$H{-}\overset{H}{\underset{H}{C}}{}^{\delta+}{-}Cl^{\delta-}$$

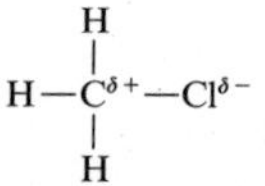

This 'pull' of electrons towards the chlorine atom is called the inductive effect. If a group attracts electrons it is said to have a −I effect e.g. Cl whereas if it tends to push electrons way it has a +I effect.

Hydrocarbons:

Alkanes

PREPARATION

(i) from the sodium salt of the carboxylic acid.

$$R[COONa + NaO]H \xrightarrow[\text{soda lime}]{\text{heat}} RH + Na_2CO_3$$

(ii) by reduction of an alkyl halide.

$$RX + [H] \rightarrow RH + HX$$

The nascent hydrogen may be produced from the action of ethanol on a zinc copper couple. Many other methods are available.

PROPERTIES

The lower alkanes tend to be inert but can be chlorinated in ultraviolet light. A mixture of substitution products is formed.

Alkenes

$>C{=}C<$ unsaturated. $CH_2{=}CH_2$ ethene. $CH_3CH{=}CH_2$ propene. $CH_3CH_2CH{=}CH_2$ but-1-ene.

PREPARATION

(i) Dehydration of an alcohol.

$$RCH_2CH_2OH \rightarrow RCH{=}CH_2 + H_2O$$

Pass alcohol vapour over hot pumice at 400°C.

(ii) from alkyl halides.

$$RCH_2CH_2Br + \underset{\text{alc.}}{\underset{\text{hot}}{KOH}} \rightarrow RCH{=}CH_2 + KBr + H_2O$$

PROPERTIES

(i) Hydrogenation to give the alkane.

$$RCH{=}CH_2 + H_2 \xrightarrow[\text{Ni cat.}]{150°C} RCH_2CH_2$$

(ii) **with halogen acids** to form alkyl halides.

$$RCH{=}CH_2 + HI \rightarrow \underset{I}{RCH}.CH_3$$

N.B. Addition is in accordance with **Markownikoff's rule** which states that the halogen atom adds to the carbon atom carrying the smaller number of hydrogen atoms.
Hydrogen iodide adds on most easily of the hydrogen halides.

(iii) **with halogens**
$RCH{=}CH_2 + Br_2 \rightarrow RCHBr.CH_2Br$

Bromine water is decolourised by olefines.

(iv) **oxidation**
Cold aq. potassium permanganate solution oxidises olefine to dihydric alcohols e.g.:
$CH_2{=}CH_2 + H_2O + [O] \rightarrow CH_2OH.CH_2OH$
ethene ethane-1, 2-diol

Ethene is oxidised by air in the presence of silver to give ethylene oxide.

$$CH_2{=}CH_2 + O_2 \rightarrow CH_2{-}CH_2 \text{ (with O bridging the two } CH_2\text{)}$$

(v) **hydration**
This may be brought about indirectly by dissolving the alkene in concentrated sulphuric acid and then diluting and warming.

$$RCH{=}CH_2 + H_2SO_4 \rightarrow \underset{\displaystyle OSO_3H}{RCH}{-}CH_3 \xrightarrow{+H_2O} \underset{\displaystyle OH}{RCH}{-}CH_3$$

(vi) **oxo process**
When carbon monoxide, hydrogen and olefines are heated under pressure aldehydes are produced which can then be reduced to alcohols.
$RCH{=}CH_2 + CO + H_2 \rightarrow RCH_2CH_2CHO$

(vii) **with ozone**

e.g.: $H_2C{=}CH_2 + O_3 \rightarrow H_2C \langle {}^{O}_{O-O} \rangle CH_2$

ethylene ozonide

If the ozonide is then hydrolysed by water, formaldehyde (methanal) is formed. Zinc is added to decompose the hydrogen peroxide which is also produced as this would oxidise the formaldehyde.

$$H_2C\langle O, O{-}O\rangle CH_2 + H_2O \rightarrow 2HCHO + H_2O_2$$

(viii) **polymerization**
Ethylene polymerizes to form polyethylene or polythene. In the Ziegler process a relatively low pressure (about 10 atmospheres) and temperature (70°C) are used together with a catalyst of an aluminium alkyl to which titanium tetrachloride has been added.

$$nCH_2{=}CH_2 \rightarrow (-CH_2{-}CH_2-)_n$$

CHART DRAWN UP FOR PROPENE

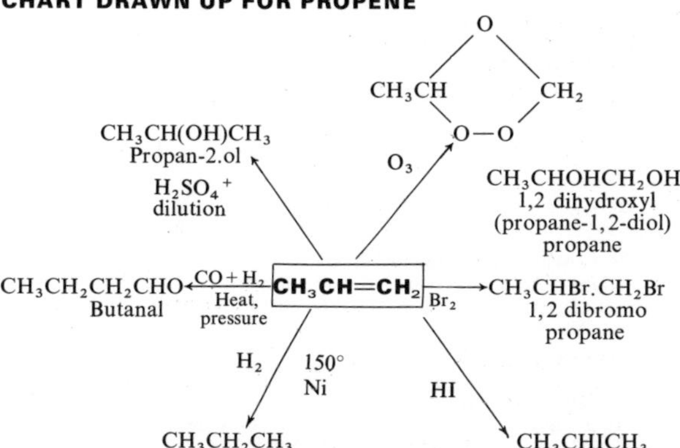

Go through this carefully and then try (from memory) to do a similar chart for but-1-ene and write in the reaction conditions. **This type of work should be carried out at the end of every homologous series.**

Alkynes

Ethyne $H—C\equiv C—H$ (Acetylene).
$CH_3CH_2—C\equiv CH$ but-1-yne
Propyne $CH_3—C\equiv CH$ (Methyl acetylene).

PREPARATION

(i) Action of cold water on calcium carbide.
$CaC_2 + 2H_2O \rightarrow Ca(OH)_2 + C_2H_2\uparrow$

(ii) From 1,2-dibromo ethane using hot alcoholic potash.
$BrCH_2.CH_2Br + KOH \rightarrow BrCH{=}CH_2 + KBr + H_2O$
$BrCH{=}CH_2 + KOH \rightarrow HC\equiv CH\uparrow + KBr + H_2O$

PROPERTIES

(i) **Burns in air** with a smoky flame.

(ii) **Hydrogenation.**

$$H—C{=}C—H \xrightarrow[150°\,Ni]{H_2} H_2C{=}CH_2 \rightarrow CH_3{\cdot}CH_3$$

cat

ethyne ethene ethane

(iii) **Halogen acids**
e.g. $HC{=}CH + HI \rightarrow H_2C{=}CHI \xrightarrow{HI} CH_3CHI_2$
1,1-di.iodoethane

(iv) **Conversion to acetaldehyde**
If acetylene is bubbled through dilute sulphuric acid at 60–80°C in the presence of mercuric sulphate as a catalyst acetaldehyde is produced.
$C_2H_2 + H_2O \rightarrow CH_3CHO$

(v) **Polymerization**

(a) if passed through a heated tube, some benzene is formed.
$3C_2H_2 \rightarrow C_6H_6$

(b) if passed into aqueous solutions of complexes of copper I chloride, vinyl acetylene is produced.
$H—C\equiv C—H + H—C\equiv C—H \rightarrow H_2C{=}CH—C\equiv CH$

This reacts with hydrogen chloride to form chloroprene which can be polymerized to form neoprene (synthetic rubber).

(vi) **Formation of metal derivatives**
e.g.: with an ammoniacal solution of copper I chloride, a red precipitate

of copper acetylide is formed.

$Cu_2Cl_2 + C_2H_2 + 2NH_3 \rightarrow Cu_2C_2 + 2NH_4Cl$

Aromatic Systems

Benzene

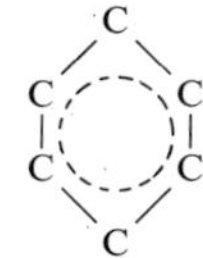

The dotted lines represent six electrons which are **delocalized**

Molecular Formula C_6H_6

Benzene cannot be represented by one simple structure because it is found that for benzene and related compounds (i) all six carbon atoms are chemically identical. (ii) that while benzene is unsaturated it is less unsaturated than would be expected of a compound containing three double bonds, e.g. compared to ethene, it does not react additively with H_2SO_4, HNO_3, etc. (iii) the bond lengths between the carbon atoms are equal, (v) the benzene nucleus is very stable and can only be broken up under extreme conditions.

PROPERTIES

(i) **Substitution reactions.** Benzene reacts with (a) **conc. sulphuric acid** under reflux to form benzene suplphonic acid:
$C_6H_6 + H_2SO_4 \rightarrow C_6H_5SO_3H + H_2O$
(b) **a mixture of concentrated nitric and sulphuric acids** below 50°C to form nitro benzene (above 50°C dinitrobenzene is formed):
$C_6H_6 + HNO_3 \rightarrow C_6H_5NO_2 + H_2O$
(c) **chlorine** at room temperatures in the presence of iron filings or iodine (called halogen carriers) to form chlorobenzene:
$C_6H_6 + Cl_2 \rightarrow C_6H_5Cl + HCl$
(d) **Alkyl halides** with anhydrous aluminium chloride as a catalyst to form higher members of the aromatic hydrocarbons:
$C_6H_6 + CH_3I \rightarrow C_6H_5CH_3 + HI$

(ii) **Addition reactions.** Benzene reacts with (a) **hydrogen** at 150°C with a nickel catalyst to form cyclohexane (a cyclic aliphatic compound): $C_6H_6 + 3H_2 \rightarrow C_6H_{12}$
(b) **chlorine** in UV light to form benzene hexachloride: $C_6H_6 + 3Cl_2 \rightarrow C_6H_6Cl_6$

Toluene $C_6H_5CH_3$

PREPARATION

(i) By reacting benzene with mono chloro methane and anhydrous aluminium chloride:
$C_6H_6 + CH_3Cl \rightarrow C_6H_5CH_3 + HCl$
(ii) By refluxing iodo-benzene iodide and sodium in dry ether:
$C_6H_5I + CH_3I + 2Na \rightarrow C_6H_5CH_3 + 2NaI$

PROPERTIES

Toluene is a colourless liquid insoluble in water B.pt 110°C. It burns to form carbon dioxide, water and soot. Like benzene toluene undergoes substitution reactions with sulphuric acid, nitric acid and chlorine. This time, however, because the methyl radical is ortho and para directing, there will be a mixture of these derivatives as the products, e.g. with sulphuric acid, ortho and para toluene sulphonic acids are formed.
Toluene also undergoes addition reactions with hydrogen but not with chlorine. Since toluene contains the methyl radical this is susceptible to attack and it will react with (i) **oxidising agents** to form either benzaldehyde or benzoic acid:

$C_6H_5CH_3 + 2[O] \rightarrow C_6H_5CHO + H_2O$
$C_6H_5CH_3 + 3[O] \rightarrow C_6H_5COOH + H_2O$

(ii) **chlorine,** providing the toluene is boiling, to produce benzyl chloride, benzal chloride and benzo-trichloride

$C_6H_5CH_3 + Cl_2 \rightarrow C_6H_5CH_2Cl$
benzyl chloride

Hydroxy Compounds

ALCOHOLS

General methods of preparation

1. Hydrolysis of alkyl halide.
   $RX + KOH_{(aq)} \rightarrow ROH + KX$
2. Reduction of aldehydes give primary alcohols.
   $RCHO + 2[H] \rightarrow RCH_2OH$

Nascent hydrogen produced by sodium amalgam and water. Alternatively reduction can be carried out by passing the aldehyde vapour and hydrogen over a metal catalyst.

3. From olefines.

$RCH{=}CH_2 + H_2SO_4 \rightarrow RCH_2CH_2HSO_4 \xrightarrow{H_2O} RCH_2CH_2OH + H_2SO_4$

Summary of Reactions of Primary Alcohols

1. **Oxidation.**

$$RCH_2OH \xrightarrow[K_2Cr_2O_7/H_2SO_4]{[O]} RCHO \xrightarrow[\text{oxidising agent}]{\text{Reflux +}} RCOOH$$

2. **Dehydration to alkenes.**

$$RCH_2CH_2OH \xrightarrow[\text{vapour over hot pumice } 400°C]{\text{Pass alcohol}} RCH{=}CH_2 + H_2O$$

3. **Ester formation.**

$$\underset{\text{acid}}{RCOOH} + \underset{\text{alcohol}}{R'CH_2OH} \underset{\text{catalyst}}{\overset{H^+}{\longleftrightarrow}} \underset{\text{ester}}{RCOOCH_2R'} + \underset{\text{water}}{H_2O}$$

4. **Formation of alkyl halides.**

$$RCH_2OH + PCl_5 \rightarrow RCH_2Cl + POCl_3 + HCl$$

To make an alkyl bromide, $NaBr + H_2SO_4$ used. Red $P + I_2$ are used to make the iodide.

5. **With concentrated sulphuric acid.**
   (a) excess acid 160° → alkene
   $RCH_2CH_2OH + H_2SO_4 \rightarrow RCH_2CH_2HSO_4 + H_2O$

$$RCH_2CH_2HSO_4 \rightarrow RCH{=}CH_2 + H_2SO_4$$

Methanol does not undergo this reaction.

(b) excess alcohol 140° → ether

$$2RCH_2OH \rightarrow RCH_2.O.CH_2R + H_2O$$

6. **With sodium** an alkoxide is formed.

$$2RCH_2OH + 2Na - 2RCH_2ONa + H_2$$

Secondary and Tertiary Alcohols

$$\begin{array}{c} R \\ \diagdown \\ \quad CHOH \\ \diagup \\ R \end{array} \qquad\qquad \begin{array}{c} R \\ \diagdown \\ R{-}C.OH \\ \diagup \\ R \end{array}$$

Secondary alcohol — Tertiary alcohol

e.g.

$$\begin{array}{c} CH_3.CHOH \\ | \\ CH_3 \end{array} \qquad\qquad \begin{array}{c} CH_3.COH.CH_3 \\ | \\ CH_3 \end{array}$$

propan-2-ol — 2-methyl propan-2-ol

Secondary and tertiary alcohols show the characteristic properties of the hydroxyl group. Secondary alcohols are oxidized to ketones

$$\rangle CHOH + [O] \rightarrow \rangle C{=}O + H_2O$$

Such a reaction necessitates the presence of an α hydrogen atom. Since tertiary alcohols do not possess this they are oxidised only with difficulty.

PHENOLS

Preparation

Sodium hydroxide and sodium benzene sulphonate are fused together in a nickel crucible at 250°C the phenol being liberated with sulphuric acid:

$$C_6H_5SO_3Na + 2NaOH \rightarrow C_6H_5ONa + Na_2SO_3 + H_2O$$
$$C_6H_5SO_3Na + H_2SO_4 \rightarrow C_6H_5OH + NaHSO_4$$

Properties

Phenol is a white, crystalline compound becoming pink on exposure to air, insoluble to water. It reacts in two ways:

1. **Those reactions due to the OH group.** It is a very weak acid and so forms salts with alkalis. The greater acidity of the hydroxyl

group in phenol may be explained in terms of one of the non bonding pairs of electrons of the oxygen atom in phenol being delocalized and becoming part of the delocalized system of electrons in the ring. Thus electrons are drawn away from the hydroxyl group facilitating the loss of a proton. **The OH group may be replaced by:**

(a) **Cl atom** using phosphorus V chloride to form a poor yield of chloro benzene:

$C_6H_5OH + PCl_5 \rightarrow C_6H_5Cl + POCl_3 + HCl$

(b) **H atom** to form benzene by heating phenol vapour with zinc dust:
$C_6H_5OH + Zn \rightarrow C_6H_6 + ZnO$
The H atom of the OH group may be replaced by:

(a) **acetyl group** to form phenyl acetate with acetyl chloride:
$C_6H_5OH + CH_3COCl \rightarrow CH_3COOC_6H_5 + HCl$

(b) **benzoyl group** to form phenyl benzoate with benzoyl chloride
$C_6H_5OH + C_6H_5COCl \rightarrow C_6H_5COOC_6H_5 + HCl$

(c) **an alkyl group** to form ethers with alkaline alkyl halides e.g. with iodo-methane, anisole is formed:
$C_6H_5ONa + CH_3I \rightarrow C_6H_5OCH_3 + NaI$

2. Those reactions due to the benzene ring. The OH group is ortho and para directing and phenol reacts with:
(a) **dilute nitric acid** to form ortho and para nitro phenol:
$C_6H_5OH + HNO_3 \rightarrow C_6H_4OH.NO_2 + H_2O$

(b) **chloromethane** in the presence of $AlCl_3$ to form ortho and para cresols:
$C_6H_5OH + CH_3Cl \rightarrow CH_3.C_6H_4.OH + HCl$

(c) **bromine water** to form 2.4.6. tribromo phenol:

Br Br

$C_6H_5OH + 3Br_2 \rightarrow$ [benzene ring] $+ 3HBr$

Br

Phenol can be reduced by hydrogen to form aliphatic cyclohexanol:
$C_6H_5OH + 3H_2 \rightarrow C_6H_{11}OH$
Note: When one drop of phenol is added to five drops of aq. iron III chloride, a violet coloration is produced.

Halides

Alkyl halides	CH_3CH_2Cl	chloroethane (ethyl chloride)
	$CH_3CHBrCH_3$	2-bromopropane
Aryl halides	C_6H_5Br (Br on benzene ring)	bromobenzene
Side chain substitution	$C_6H_5CH_2Cl$ (CH_2Cl on benzene ring)	benzyl chloride or chlorotoluene

Preparation

1. From alcohols.
   (a) $ROH + HBr \xrightarrow{\text{reflux}} RBr + H_2O$ Phenols do not react in this way.
   (b) $ROH + PCl_5 \rightarrow RCl + POCl_3 + HCl$
   With PCl_5 phenol gives a poor yield of chlorobenzene.
2. Aromatic diazonium salts react with chloride or bromide ions in the presence of a copper catalyst.
$C_6H_5N_2{}^+ + Cl^- \rightarrow C_6H_5Cl + N_2$
No catalyst is required for the reaction with iodide ion.

Properties

1. With nucleophilic reagents

(a) $RBr + CN^- \rightarrow RCN + Br^-$
alc.
(b) $RBr + OH^- \rightarrow ROH + Br^-$
(c) $RBr + I^- \rightarrow RI + Br^-$
this reaction is usually carried out in acetone.
(d) $RBr + NH_3 \rightarrow RNH_3{}^+ + Br^-$
(e) with alcoholic solutions of an alkoxide, ethers are formed:
$C_2H_5Br + C_2H_5O \rightarrow C_2H_5OC_2H_5 + Br^-$

Iodides are the most reactive, chlorides the least. Aryl halides are unreactive and require more extreme conditions e.g. chlorobenzene is hydrolysed by aq. sodium hydroxide only at about 350°C and under considerable pressure. However side chain substitution products are extremely reactive.

2. With metals

(a) in dry ethereal solutions, alkyl and aryl halides (except aryl chloride) react with magnesium to form Grignard reagents e.g.

$C_2H_5Br + Mg \rightarrow C_2H_5MgBr$ (ethyl magnesium bromide)

(b) with sodium in dry ethereal solution—WURTZ reaction

$R_1I + R_2I + 2Na \rightarrow R_1R_2 + 2NaI$

An alkane is formed.

Fittig reaction—one halide is aryl and one alkyl.

e.g. $C_6H_5Br + C_2H_5Br + 2Na \rightarrow C_6H_5C_2H_5 + 2NaBr$ (ethyl benzene)

3. ester formation

with silver salts of carboxylic acids, esters are formed.

e.g. $RCOOAg + R'I \rightarrow RCOOR' + AgI$

4. with silver cyanide

$RBr + AgCN \rightarrow RNC + AgBr$ (iso-cyanide)

REACTION OF GRIGNARD REAGENTS

1. If solid carbon dioxide is added to a cold solution of the Grignard reagent and the mixture acidified, a carboxylic acid is formed.

$$R{-}Mg{-}I \xrightarrow{CO_2} R{-}\overset{\overset{O}{\|}}{C}{-}O{-}MgI \xrightarrow[H_2O]{H^+} R\overset{\overset{O}{\|}}{C}{-}OH + Mg(OH)I$$

2. Water, alcohols and carboxylic acids react with Grignard reagents to form hydrocarbons.

$R{-}Mg{-}I + H_2O \rightarrow RH + MgIOH$

3. With formaldehyde, a primary alcohol is formed

$$R{-}Mg{-}I \xrightarrow{H.CHO} (R)(H)C(OMgI)(H) \xrightarrow[H_2O]{H^+} RCH_2OH + Mg(OH)I$$

4. With other aldehydes a secondary alcohol is produced.

$$R{-}MgI \xrightarrow{R^1CHO} (R)(R^1)C(OMgI)(H) \longrightarrow (R)(R^1)CHOH + Mg(OH)I$$

Amines

CH_3NH_2 Methylamine (aminomethane) $C_2H_5NH_2$ ethylamine (aminoethane) $C_6H_5NH_2$ aniline (amino benzene).
These are primary amines but if other alkyl or aryl groups are substituted for the hydrogen atom e.g. $(CH_3)_2NH$, $(CH_3)_3N$ these are known as secondary and tertiary amines respectively.

Preparation

(a) Aliphatic primary amines

1. Reduction of alkyl cyanide or acid amide.

$RCN + 4[H] \rightarrow RCH_2NH_2$

2. By reacting an amide with bromide and an alkali.

(b) Aniline $C_6H_5NH_2$

By reducing nitrobenzene with nascent hydrogen produced by the action of concentrated hydrochloric acid on tin:

$C_6H_5NO_2 + 6[H] \rightarrow C_6H_5NH_2 + 2H_2O$

Aniline remains in solution as aniline hydrochloride:

$C_6H_5NH_2 + HCl \rightarrow C_6H_5NH_3{}^+Cl^-$

Excess sodium hydroxide solution is added to liberate free aniline which is then removed by steam distillation:

$$C_6H_5NH_3{}^+Cl^- + NaOH \rightarrow C_6H_5NH_2 + NaCl + H_2O$$

Properties

1. Basicity

Aliphatic amines are more basic than ammonia but aromatic amines are less basic than ammonia.

$$RNH_2 + H_2O \rightarrow RNH_3{}^+ + OH^-$$

In an aliphatic amine the small inductive effect of the alkyl group gives a slight increase of basicity compared with ammonia e.g.

$$CH_3CH_2CH_2 \rightarrow N\begin{matrix} \diagup H \\ \diagdown H \end{matrix}$$

In aniline the electron pair of the nitrogen atom becomes involved in the delocalized system of electrons in the benzene ring and thus the basicity is reduced:

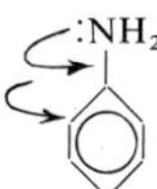

2. Acylation i.e. replacement of a hydrogen atom of the $-NH_2$ group by an acyl radical R′CO. e.g. acetylation of ethylamine to give N—acetylethylamine:

$C_2H_5NH_2 + CH_3CONH_2 \rightarrow C_2H_5NHCOCH_3 + HCl\uparrow$

benzyolation of aniline to give benzanilide
$C_6H_5NH_2 + C_6H_5COCl \rightarrow C_6H_5NHCOC_6H_5 + HCl\uparrow$

3. Carbylamine reaction forming an isocyanide (vile smell)
$RNH_2 + CHCl_3 + 3KOH \rightarrow RNC + 3KCl + 3H_2O$

4. Nitrous acid (sodium nitrite + hydrochloric acid).
(a) primary aliphatic amines, aromatic amine $>10°C$
$RNH_2 + HONO \rightarrow ROH + N_2\uparrow + H_2O$
(b) aromatic amines $<10°C$
$C_6H_5NH_2 + H^+ + HONO \rightarrow C_6H_5N^+ \equiv N + 2H_2O$
A phenyl diazonium salt is formed.

PROPERTIES OF DIAZONIUM SALTS

1. Where the N_2Cl group is replaced by:
(a) a hydroxide group to form phenol when the solution is boiled:
$C_6H_5N_2Cl + H_2O \rightarrow C_6H_5OH + N_2\uparrow + HCl$
(b) halogen atom when (i) copper I halide is added dissolved in the concentrated halogen acid:
$C_6H_4N_2Cl + CuBr \rightarrow C_6H_5Br + N_2\uparrow + CuCl$
(ii) finely divided copper is added:
$C_6H_5N_2Cl \rightarrow C_6H_5Cl + N_2\uparrow$
(iii) boiling potassium iodide solution is added:
$C_6H_5N_2Cl + KI \rightarrow C_6H_5I + N_2\uparrow + KCl$
(c) a cyanide group to form phenyl cyanide by treating the solution with copper I cyanide dissolved in aq. potassium cyanide:
$C_6H_5N_2Cl + KCN \rightarrow C_6H_5CN + N_2\uparrow + KCl$

2. Coupling reaction to give brightly coloured compounds.
(a) dimethylaniline to form p-dimethylamino azo benzene (yellow):
$C_6H_5N_2{}^+Cl^- + C_6H_5N(CH_3)_2 \rightarrow C_6H_5N{=}NC_6H_5N(CH_3)_2 + HCl\uparrow$
(b) phenol to form para-hydroxyazobenzene (orange):
$C_6H_5N_2{}^+Cl^- + C_6H_5OH \rightarrow C_6H_5N{=}N{-}C_6H_4OH + HCl\uparrow$

Aldehydes and Ketones

Preparation

1. Aldehydes are made by the oxidation of primary alcohols and ketones by the oxidation of secondary alcohols. The oxidising agent is acidified potassium dichromate.

$$RCH_2OH + [O] \rightarrow \underset{\text{aldehyde}}{RCHO} + H_2O$$

$$R(R^1)CHOH + [O] \rightarrow R(R^1)C{=}O + H_2O$$

2. Both may be made by heating the anhydrous calcium salts of carboxylic acids. Poor yields are obtained.

e.g. $(CH_3COO)_2Ca \rightarrow CH_3COCH_3 + CaCO_3$

$(C_6H_5COO)_2Ca \rightarrow C_6H_5COC_6H_5 + CaCO_3$

3. Oxidation of aromatic side chains e.g. toluene is oxidised to benzaldehyde by chromyl chloride.

$C_6H_5CH_3 + 2[O] \rightarrow C_6H_5CHO + H_2O$

Properties

1. Aldehydes are reducing agents and reduce (a) Fehling's solution to copper I oxide (red precipitate) (b) ammoniacal silver nitrate to silver (silver mirror).

2. Reduction with hydrogen Aldehydes form primary alcohols ketones give secondary alcohols. Hydrogen may be used in the presence of a nickel catalyst.

$RCHO + H_2 \rightarrow RCH_2OH : RCOR' + H_2 \rightarrow RCHOHR'$

3. With ammonia Complex reactions occur (a) some aldehydes form simple addition compounds e.g. acetaldehyde forms acetaldehyde ammonia.

$$CH_3C(H){=}O + NH_3 \rightarrow CH_3{-}C(H)(NH_2){-}OH$$

However this simple product rapidly polymerizes and more complex products are formed. (b) Formaldehyde and benzaldehyde condense to give more complex products. Formaldehyde yields hexamethylene tetramine

$6HCHO + 4NH_3 \rightarrow (CH_2)_6N_4 + 6H_2O$

Benzaldehyde forms hydrobenzamide.

4. With HCN, $NaHSO_3$

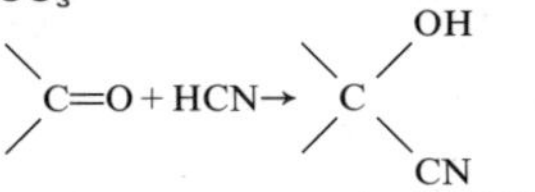

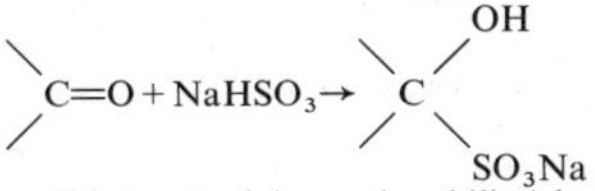

$$\rangle C{=}O + HCN \rightarrow \rangle C \langle^{OH}_{CN}$$

$$\rangle C{=}O + NaHSO_3 \rightarrow \rangle C \langle^{OH}_{SO_3Na}$$

The carbon atom is susceptible to attack by nucleophilic (electron donor) reagents because of the polarity

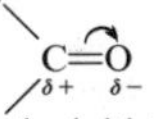

$$\rangle \overset{\delta+}{C}{=}\overset{\delta-}{O}$$

The reaction probably proceeds by initial attack by the cyanide ion

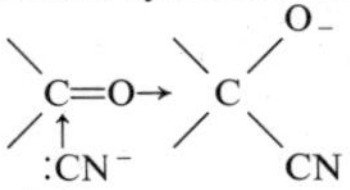

$$\underset{:CN^-}{\rangle C{=}O} \rightarrow \rangle C \langle^{O^-}_{CN}$$

and then addition of a proton

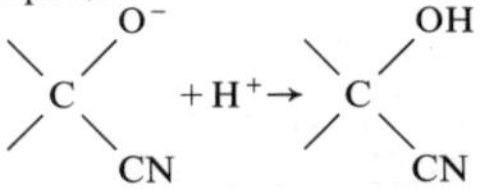

$$\rangle C \langle^{O^-}_{CN} + H^+ \rightarrow \rangle C \langle^{OH}_{CN}$$

The compounds formed are cyanohydrins, which are easily hydrolysed to hydroxy acids e.g. acetaldehyde cyanohydrin forms lactic acid (hydroxy propionic acid).

5. Reaction with hydroxylamine, hydrazine etc.

(a) with hydroxylamine, an oxime is formed

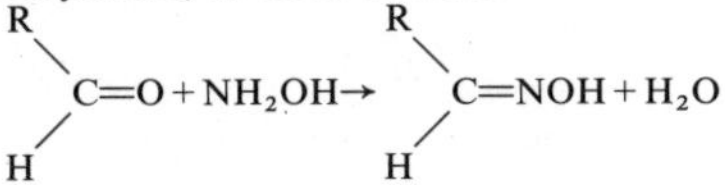

$$\overset{R}{\underset{H}{\rangle}} C{=}O + NH_2OH \rightarrow \overset{R}{\underset{H}{\rangle}} C{=}NOH + H_2O$$

an aldoxime

(b) with hydrazine and phenylhydrazine, hydrazones and phenylhydrazones are formed.

2.4 dinitrophenylhydrazine $NO_2{-}C_6H_3(NO_2){-}NHNH_2$

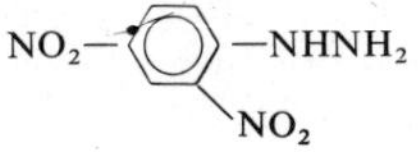

produces crystalline products which are easily purified and have sharp melting points. They can therefore be used to identify carbonyl compounds.

6. Oxidation Mild oxidising agents e.g. acidified sodium dichromate convert aldehydes to carboxylic acids.

$RCHO + [O] \rightarrow RCOOH$

Ketones are oxidised with difficulty and the resulting carboxylic acid contains fewer carbon atoms than the ketone from which it was formed.

7. Aldol condensation (a) in the presence of dilute alkali, acetaldehyde reacts to give aldol.

$2CH_3CHO \rightarrow CH_3CHOH.CH_2CHO$

only aldehydes with α-hydrogen atoms can undergo this reaction. Ketones can condense in this way but the reaction is reversible.

$2CH_3COCH_3 \rightleftharpoons (CH_3)_2COHCH_2COCH_3$

(b) benzaldehyde undergoes analagous reactions e.g., Claison reaction—in the presence of alkali, benzaldehyde and acetaldehyde react to give cinnamic aldehyde.

$C_6H_5CHO + CH_3CHO \rightarrow C_6H_5CH{=}CHCHO + H_2O$

8. Cannizzaro reaction Aldehydes with no α-hydrogen atoms disproportionate in the presence of caustic alkali e.g.

(i) formaldehyde reacts to form methanol and sodium formate
$2HCHO + NaOH \rightarrow CH_3OH + HCOONa$

(ii) benzaldehyde forms sodium benzoate and benzyl alcohol.
$2C_6H_5CHO + NaOH \rightarrow C_6H_5COONa + C_6H_5CH_2OH$

9. Acetal formation Aldehydes react with alcohols to form a hemiacetal in solution. In the presence of H^+ (catalyst) hemiacetal react with a further molecule of alcohol to form acetals

$$\begin{matrix} R \\ H \end{matrix}\!\!>\!C{=}O + R^1OH \rightarrow \begin{matrix} R \\ H \end{matrix}\!\!>\!C\!<\!\!\begin{matrix} OH \\ OR^1 \end{matrix} \quad \text{a hemiacetal}$$

$$\begin{matrix} R \\ H \end{matrix}\!\!>\!C\!<\!\!\begin{matrix} OH \\ OR^1 \end{matrix} + R^1OH \rightarrow \begin{matrix} R \\ H \end{matrix}\!\!>\!C\!<\!\!\begin{matrix} OR^1 \\ OR^1 \end{matrix} + H_2O$$

an acetal

10. Polymerization Ketones and aromatic aldehydes do not polymerize. Acetaldehyde polymerizes to form

(i) paraldehyde $(CH_3CHO)_3$ on treatment with a few drops of concentrated sulphuric acid (ii) metaldehyde $(CH_3CHO)_4$ in the presence of dry hydrogen chloride at 0°C.

Carboxylic Acids

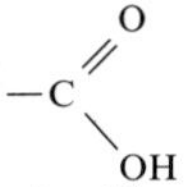

$$-C\begin{smallmatrix}\diagup\!\!\!\diagup O \\ \diagdown OH\end{smallmatrix}$$

H.COOH formic acid (methanoic acid).
CH_3COOH acetic acid (ethanoic acid).
C_2H_5COOH propionic acid (propanoic acid).
C_6H_5COOH benzoic acid.

PREPARATION

1. Oxidation of primary alcohols or aldehydes by refluxing with acidified sodium dichromate solution.
$RCH_2OH + 2[O] \rightarrow RCOOH + H_2O$
2. Hydrolysis of a cyanide with dilute hydrochloric acid.
$RCN + 2H_2O + HCl \rightarrow RCOOH + NH_4Cl$
Benzoic acid can be prepared by oxidising toluene with an alkaline solution of potassium permanganate.
$C_6H_5CH_3 + 3[O] \rightarrow C_6H_5COOH + H_2O$

PROPERTIES

1. Acid behaviour Carboxylic acids are acidic yet alcohols are not although both contain the $-OH$ group. The electronegative oxygen atom of the carboxyl group tends to pull electrons toward itself from the carbon atom (inductive effect) and in turn the pair of electrons bonding the oxygen and hydrogen atoms of the $-OH$ is withdrawn towards the carbon atom making the hydrogen atom more available to a base. There is also delocalization of electrons.

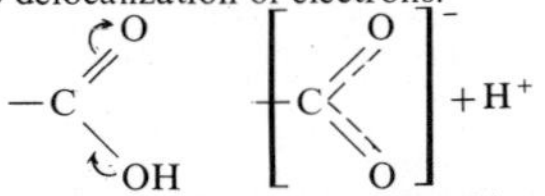

$$-C\begin{smallmatrix}\diagup\!\!\!\diagup O \\ \diagdown OH\end{smallmatrix} \quad \left[-C\begin{smallmatrix}O \\ O\end{smallmatrix}\right]^- + H^+$$

Chloroacetic acid is a stronger acid than acetic acid and the strength of the chloroacetic acid increases with the number of chlorine atoms. The chlorine atom also attracts electrons ($-I$ effect) making it easier for the hydrogen atom of the carboxyl group to be lost to a base.
Aromatic acids are stronger than fatty acids.

2. Carboxylic acids react with alcohols to form esters.
$ROH + R'COOH \rightleftharpoons R'COOR + H_2O$

3. Phosphorus pentachloride to form acid chlorides.
$RCOOH + PCl_5 \rightarrow RCOCl + POCl_3 + HCl$

4. Chlorine in the presence of sunlight or a catalyst such as red phosphorus to undergo substitution reactions with those hydrogens attached to the carbon atom adjacent to the carboxyl group
e.g. $RCH_2COOH + Cl_2 \rightarrow RCHClCOOH + HCl$
5. Dehydrating agents to give acid anhydrides.

DERIVATIVES OF CARBOXYLIC ACIDS

Esters

Methyl formate $HCOOCH_3$.
Ethyl benzoate $C_6H_5COOC_2H_5$.
Methyl acetate CH_3COOCH_3.

Preparation

1. By refluxing a carboxylic acid and an alcohol in the presence of a small quantity of concentrated sulphuric acid which acts as a catalyst and a dehydrating agent, e.g. methyl alcohol and acetic acid to give methyl acetate.
$CH_3OH + CH_3COOH \rightleftharpoons CH_3COOCH_3 + H_2O$
Esters made from formic acid cannot be prepared by this method since the acid would be dehydrated by the sulphuric acid and therefore these esters are usually made by the following methods.
2. By refluxing an alkyl halide with the silver salt of a carboxylic acid. e.g. ethyl iodide with silver acetate to give ethyl acetate.
$C_2H_5I + CH_3COOAg \rightarrow CH_3COOC_2H_5 + AgI$
3. By refluxing the acid with an alcohol saturated with hydrogen chloride.
$CH_3OH + HCOOH \rightleftharpoons HCOOCH_3 + H_2O$
4. By reacting an alcohol with an acid chloride or an acid anhydride, e.g. methyl alcohol and acetyl chloride to give methyl acetate.
$CH_3OH + CH_3COCl \rightarrow CH_3COOCH_3 + HCl$

Properties Esters are liquids with pleasant smells and only lightly soluble in water. Esters react with (i) boiling dilute mineral acids to give an acid plus an alcohol e.g. methyl acetate to give methyl alcohol and acetic acid
$CH_3COOCH + H_2O \rightleftharpoons CH_3OH + CH_3COOH$

(ii) boiling dilute alkalis to give sodium salt of the acid and an alcohol. This is called saponification:

$$C_6H_5COOC_2H_5 + NaOH \rightarrow C_6H_5COONa + C_2H_5OH$$

(iii) ammonia to form acid amides and an alcohol, e.g. methyl acetate to give acetamide and methyl alcohol:

$$CH_3COOCH_3 + NH_3 \rightarrow CH_3CONH_2 + CH_3OH$$

(iv) nascent hydrogen to form alcohols e.g. ethyl acetate forms ethanol.

$$CH_3COOC_2H_5 + 4[H] \rightarrow 2C_2H_5OH$$

(v) phosphorus pentachloride to give acid chlorides e.g. ethyl acetate gives acetyl chloride:

$$CH_3COOC_2H_5 + PCl_5 \rightarrow CH_3COCl + POCl_3 + C_2H_5Cl$$

ACID CHLORIDES

$-C(=O)Cl$ Acetyl chloride $CH_3C(=O)Cl$; benzoyl chloride $C_6H_5C(=O)Cl$

Preparation

By the action of thionyl chloride (useful as other products are gaseous) or phosphorus pentachloride.

$$CH_3COOH + SOCl_2 \rightarrow CH_3COCl + SO_2\uparrow + HCl\uparrow$$
$$C_6H_5COOH + PCl_5 \rightarrow C_6H_5COCl + POCl_3 + HCl\uparrow$$

Properties

The acid chlorides are colourless liquids with irritating smells, fuming in moist air. Acid chlorides are very reactive and react:
(i) with water to give acids and hydrogen chloride (only aliphatic are violent)

$$CH_3COCl + H_2O \rightarrow CH_3COOH + HCl\uparrow$$

(ii) violently with alcohols to give esters:

$$C_6H_5COCl + C_2H_5OH \rightarrow C_6H_5COOC_2H_5 + HCl\uparrow$$

(iii) vigorously with concentrated ammonia solution to give acid amides:

$$CH_3COCl + 2NH_3 \rightarrow CH_3CONH_2 + NH_4Cl$$

with ammonia, benzoyl chloride gives benzamide $C_6H_5CONH_2$
(iv) with nascent hydrogen to give first aldehydes and then alcohols:
$CH_3COCl + 2[H] \rightarrow CH_3CHO + HCl\uparrow$
$CH_3CHO + 2[H] \rightarrow CH_3CH_2OH$

(v) with sodium salts of carboxylic acids to give acid anhydrides:

$C_6H_5COCl + CH_3COONa \rightarrow (C_6H_5CO)_2O + NaCl$
In these reactions acetyl chloride is called the acetylating agent and the reactions are known as acetylations. Benzoyl chloride is a benzyolating agent e.g.

$C_6H_5NH_2 + NaOH + Cl.CO.C_6H_5 \rightarrow C_6H_5NH.CO.C_6H_5 + NaCl + H_2O$
Aniline is benzyolated to form benzanilide.

ACID ANHYDRIDES

$$\begin{array}{l} -C\overset{\displaystyle O}{\diagup\!\!\diagup} \\ \quad\diagdown \\ \quad\; O \\ \quad\diagup \\ -C\underset{\displaystyle O}{\diagdown\!\!\diagdown} \end{array}$$

e.g. acetic anhydride $(CH_3CO)_2O$

Preparation
1. By heating sodium acetate with acetyl chloride
$CH_3COONa + CH_3COCl \rightarrow (CH_3CO)_2O + NaCl$
2. By dehydrating acetic acid
$2CH_3COOH \rightarrow (CH_3CO)_2O + H_2O$

Properties Acetic anhydride is a colourless pungent smelling liquid. It reacts with:
(i) water to form acetic acid:
$(CH_3CO)_2O + H_2O \rightarrow 2CH_3COOH$
(ii) alcohol to form ethyl acetate and acetic acid:
$(CH_3CO)_2O + C_2H_5OH \rightarrow CH_3COOC_2H_5 + CH_3COOH$
(iii) ammonia solution to form acetamide and acetic acid:
$(CH_3CO)_2O + NH_3 \rightarrow CH_3CONH_2 + CH_3COOH$
Benzoic anhydride is less reactive than acetic anhydride but is an efficient benzyolating agent.

ACID AMIDES

$$-C\begin{matrix}\nearrow O \\ \searrow NH_2\end{matrix} \quad \text{e.g. } CH_3C\begin{matrix}\nearrow O \\ \searrow NH_2\end{matrix} \quad \text{acetamide}$$

Preparation By heating ammonium acetate with glacial acetic acid:
$CH_3COONH_4 \rightarrow CH_3CONH_2 + H_2O$

Properties Acetamide is a colourless, crystalline solid soluble in water. It is a neutral substance but also amphoteric forming salts with both acids and bases. Acetamide reacts with (i) boiling dilute mineral acid to give acetic acid:
$HCl + CH_3CONH_2 + H_2O \rightarrow CH_3COOH + NH_4Cl$

(ii) boiling dilute alkali to give sodium acetate and ammonia
$CH_3CONH_2 + NaOH \rightarrow CH_3COONa + NH_3\uparrow$

(iii) phosphorus pentoxide to give methyl cyanide:
$CH_3CONH_2 \rightarrow CH_3CN + H_2O$

(iv) nitrous acid to give acetic acid and nitrogen:
$CH_3CONH_2 + HNO_2 \rightarrow CH_3COOH + N_2\uparrow + H_2O$

(v) bromine and alkali to give methylamine:
$CH_3CONH_2 + KOH + Br_2 \rightarrow CH_3CONHBr + KBr + H_2O$
$CH_3CONHBr + 3KOH \rightarrow CH_3NH_2 + KBr + K_2CO_3 + H_2O$

The properties of benzamide are very similar to those of acetamide.

NITRILES or CYANIDES

Preparation

1. Dehydration of amides with phosphorous pentoxide

$RCONH_2 \xrightarrow{P_2O_5} RCN + H_2O$

2. From alkyl halides by refluxing with an alcohol solution of potassium cyanide:

$RX + KCN \rightarrow KX + RCN$

Properties (i) hydrolysis in acid condition to form carboxylic acids:
$RCN + H_2O \rightarrow RCONH_2 \xrightarrow[H^+Cl^-]{+H_2O} RCOOH + NH_4Cl$
hydrogen or using molecular hydrogen in the presence of a nickel catalyst.
$RCN + 2H_2 \rightarrow RCH_2NH_2$

Polymers

A polymer is a large molecule formed by the linking together of smaller molecules which may be identical or different.

ADDITION POLYMERIZATION

This is the formation of a large molecule (polymer) from many small identical molecules (monomer). The simple molecules that can polymerize by this method are all unsaturated during reaction, the double bond between the carbon atoms breaks and linear polymer chains are formed. e.g. ethene

$n(CH_2{=}CH_2) \rightarrow (-CH_2-CH_2-)_n$

The linear polymer chains become entangled to form a solid polymer e.g.

Polymer	Monomer
1. P.V.C. $(-CH_2-CHCl-)_n$ poly vinyl chloride	$CH_2{=}CHCl$ vinyl chloride
2. polystyrene $\left(-CH_2-\underset{C_6H_5}{\overset{H}{C}}-\right)_n$	styrene $C_6H_5CH{=}CH_2$
3. polythene $\left(-\underset{H}{\overset{H}{C}}-\underset{H}{\overset{H}{C}}-\right)_n$	ethene $CH_2{=}CH_2$

The conditions for polymerization are usually either (i) a high pressure in the presence of a trace of oxygen or (ii) a low temperature and pressure in the presence of a **Zeigler catalyst.** This consists of a mixture of an organometalic compound such as aluminium triethyl and the halide of a transition element e.g. titanium tetrachloride.

Structure of polymers

Propene $CH_2{=}CHCH_3$ and similar molecule polymerize to give different forms. In the **Isotactic** form all the methyl groups lie on the same side of the molecule and in the **Syndiotactic** form the methyl groups are arranged on alternate sides. In a third form, the methyl groups are arranged haphazardly and this is called the **Atactic** form.

CONDENSATION POLYMERIZATION

This occurs when two types of molecule combine with the elimination of some small molecule. It is essential that each molecule is 'double-ended' i.e. the molecule must have two functional groups e.g. diols, diamines, dicarboxylic acids. When dicarboxylic acids and diols are involved the polymers are **polyesters.**

Terylene is formed from glycol $\begin{matrix} CH_2OH \\ | \\ CH_2OH \end{matrix}$ and dimethyl terephthalate.

Methanol is eliminated

$$CH_3OOC\text{—}C_6H_4\text{—}COOCH_3 + HOCH_2CH_2OH$$

$$\downarrow$$

$$CH_3OOC\text{—}C_6H_4\text{—}COOCH_2CH_2OH \quad + CH_3OH$$

A B

This molecule is then able to react with more glycol at end A and with more dimethyl terephthalate at B.

Nylon is also formed by condensation. The monomers are adipic acid $HOOC(CH_2)_4COOH$ and hexamethylene diamine $H_2N(CH_2)_6NH_2$. Water is eliminated.

$$H_2N(CH_2)_6NH_2 + HOOC(CH_2)_4COOH$$

$$\downarrow$$

$$H_2N(CH_2)_6\underset{\substack{| \\ H}}{N}OC(CH_2)_4COOH + H_2O$$

ready to react with more acid (↑ at H_2N end); ready to react with more base (↖ at COOH end)

This polymer is called **nylon 6·6** meaning that each monomer unit has 6 carbon atoms.

PROTEINS

These are polymers and amino acids are the monomer units. When two amino acids condense water is eliminated and a **dipeptide** is formed.

$$RCH(NH_2)C(=O)\text{—}OH \quad + \quad H\text{—}N(H)\text{—}C(R_2)(H)\text{—}COOH$$

$$\downarrow$$

$$RCH(NH_2)\overset{\substack{O \\ \|}}{C}\text{—}\underset{\substack{| \\ H}}{N}\text{—}\underset{\substack{| \\ H}}{\overset{\substack{R_2 \\ |}}{C}}\text{—}COOH$$

the linkage

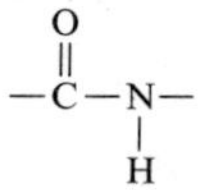

$$-\overset{\overset{\displaystyle O}{\|}}{C}-\underset{\underset{\displaystyle H}{|}}{N}-$$

is called the **peptide link.** The process is repeated many times forming polypeptides and eventually proteins. The sequence of the amino acids in the polypeptide chain is known as the **primary structure.** There are about twenty amino acids found in proteins and all except glycine are optically active. Since amino acids have two functional groups $-NH_2$ and $-COOH$ they show properties of both.

In water, the acid ionises $^{+}NH_3RCHOCOO^{-}$
in alkaline solution $NH_2RCHCOO^{-}$
and in acid solution $^{+}NH_3RCHCOOH$.

The polypeptide chain is often coiled in a form known as the α-helix and this is referred to as the **secondary structure.** The chain is held in this form by means of hydrogen bonds between the peptide links. Thus

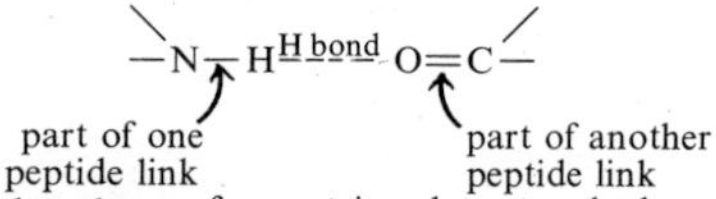

$$\diagdown N-H \overset{\text{H bond}}{- - -} O=C \diagup$$

part of one peptide link (N–H); part of another peptide link (O=C)

The tertiary structure of a protein relates to whether the protein is fibrous as in hair or globular as in egg albumin.

Separation of amino acids by chromotography

Free amino acids can be produced by hydrolysis of the protein and this is achieved by refluxing with hydrochloric acid for about 24 hours. A spot of hydrolysate is placed on a piece of chromotography paper which is dropped into a solvent such as a mixture of butan-1-ol and acetic acid. Separation depends on the relative solubility of each amino acid in the stationary solvent (water which is bonded in the cellulose fibres of the paper) and the moving solvent.

In complete separation it is then necessary to use a second solvent which is allowed to run at right angles to the direction of the first.

The amino acids are located by drying the paper in an oven and then spraying with nin hydrin solution. The paper is then heated in the oven again, when purple spots mark the position of the acid.

The Rf values of each amino acid can be measured

$$R_f \text{ value} = \frac{\text{distance moved by amino acid}}{\text{distance moved by solvent}}$$

Synthesis of Organic Compounds

To answer questions involving the synthesis of organic compounds it is essential to know:

1. methods of preparation and chief reactions of all classes of organic compounds.
2. how to ascend and descend homologous series.

In converting compound A to compound B always avoid taking a large number of stages—this leads to a poor yield and would be unnecessarily time consuming process. **For each stage name all reagents,** necessary **reaction conditions** and write an **equation** unless other instructions are given, e.g. suggest a synthetic route for converting $CH_3CO_2H \rightarrow CH_2(NH_2)CO_2H$ naming reagents to be used and stating conditions.

$$CH_3CO_2H \xrightarrow[\text{or U.V. light}]{Cl_2 \text{ red P}} \underset{\text{chloroacetic acid}}{CH_2ClCO_2H} \xrightarrow[\text{ammonia solution}]{\text{conc}} CH_2NH_2CO_2H$$

ASCENT OF THE HOMOLOGOUS SERIES

1. $ROH \xrightarrow{\text{Red } P+I_2} RI \xrightarrow{\text{alc. KCN}} RCN \xrightarrow[Na/C_2H_5OH]{[H]} RCH_2NH_2 \xrightarrow[HCl]{NaNO_2} RCH_2OH$
2. $ROH \xrightarrow{\text{Red } P+I_2} RI \xrightarrow[\text{Dry ether}]{Mg} RMgI \xrightarrow{CO_2} RCOOH \xrightarrow{C_2H_5OH} RCOOC_2H_5 \xrightarrow{LiAlH_4} RCH_2OH$

DESCENT OF A HOMOLOGOUS SERIES

$$RCH_2OH \xrightarrow{[O]} RCOOH \xrightarrow{(NH_4)_2CO_3} RCOONH_4 \xrightarrow{\text{heat}} RCONH_2$$

$$ROH \xrightarrow{NaNO_2} RNH_2 \xrightarrow[\text{Hofmann's Reaction}]{Br_2/KOH} RCONH_2$$

Complete List of Key Facts Educational Aids

KEY FACTS COURSE COMPANION BOOKS

Physics
Chemistry
Biology
Additional Mathematics
Modern Mathematics
Arithmetic and Trigonometry
Algebra
Geometry
English
Economics
French
Geography

price 55p each.

KEY FACTS CARDS

English Language and Examination Essay
English Comprehension and Precis
Geography
History
French
Biology
Chemistry
Physics
Modern Mathematics
Elementary Mathematics
Additional Mathematics
Arithmetic and Trigonometry
General Science
Economics
Geography—Regional
Algebra
Geometry
Technical Drawing
Latin
German
Macbeth
Julius Caesar
New Testament

price 50p each.

KEY FACTS 'A' LEVEL BOOKS

Pure Mathematics
Physics
Biology
Chemistry

price 55p each.

Published in Great Britain by
Intercontinental Book Productions
in conjunction with and available from
SEYMOUR PRESS LIMITED, 334 Brixton Road,
London SW9 7AG.